THROUGH
Unlocked Doors

THROUGH
Unlocked Doors

a. e. ames

Copyright © a. e. ames.

All rights reserved. No part of this book may be reproduced in any form or by any electronic or mechanical means, including information storage and retrieval systems, without permission in writing from the publisher, except by reviewers, who may quote brief passages in a review.

ISBN: 978-1-64713-520-1 (Paperback Edition)
ISBN: 978-1-64713-521-8 (Hardcover Edition)
ISBN: 978-1-64713-519-5 (E-book Edition)

Some characters and events in this book are fictitious. Any similarity to real persons, living or dead, is coincidental and not intended by the author.

Book Ordering Information

Phone Number: 347-901-4929 or 347-901-4920
Email: info@globalsummithouse.com
Global Summit House
www.globalsummithouse.com

Printed in the United States of America

Contents

Poem	Night is Black	1
Rose Quartz	Introduction	7
Oak Door	An Omen	9
Pearl Door Knob	Going to Town	11
Ruby	Priming the Pump	13
Black Onyx	Innocence	16
Poem	A Time to Cry	19
Golden Topaz	Safe Places	22
Aquamarine	The Skiff Meets the Sea	25
Silver	Contests	29
Coral	California on Call	35
	Some of the Best	37
White Quartz	Subtle Seduction	42
Blue Azure	Airborne	46
	II Honeymoon	52
Cameo	Adventure	56
Yellow Azure	The Yellow Rose	62
Diamonds	Rescued from Drowning	67
Opal	The Fall of Camelot	71
Gold	The Finale	75
Poem	I Wonder	77

Night is Black

The night, black as black is, without light
From stars, candles or lamps.

My eyes open, yet I see nothing
Late in the stillness of the hours.

Whisper, "It is time for slumber."

Ears are open, I hear nothing more.

Moving towards the bed reaching to feel
The mattress form and pillows.

I soundlessly search for a form.

Climbing into the safe place, I tug up the comforter
To cuddle with for warmth.

Back still, as I close my eyes to sleep
In the quiet of darkness.

Knowing there is nothing around but the night
My mind gives up to sleep.

Stillness lulls the brain for the rest.

Hours of slumber, sometimes dreaming, hours fly by
Then quite suddenly, a Sunbeam peaks through the window.

Good Morning! Arrives the light . . .

a e. ames

Introduction

It was one of those nostalgic days as Amelia wanted to think back on all the joys and mistakes she had made to be able to look forward again. She knew it was necessary to learn from life with an honest review that may be hurtful. At this age of nineteen, there are choices to make, like crossing over lines that molds into more maturity, shaking off fear. This had to be done alone. She realized what was passed down while driving the car and thought of what her aunt had told about her mother, Marie. It seems that her mom was a young teenage lady when a Hollywood crew came to Amity to check out locations for a movie. While in town, they noticed mom shopping. Approaching her, they were polite and inquired if she had ever acted.

"No," she replied.

They asked, "Could we visit the parents to speak to them?"

Gleefully, she said, "Well, yes!"

When Mom's parents, grandma and grandpa, heard their proposal, they refused. The director left, and Marie pitched a fit and had to be confined to her room to calm down. She never forgot her disappointment in her entire life. Hence there was always, her daughter. Marie could see how she was developing into a pretty, personable child and envisioned her growing up into a beautiful young woman. Amelia was growing tall with long legs like her Dad. Her big blue eyes, blonde hair and winning smile, her own. Marie would pave the way for her to have the opportunities Marie did not have. She smiled to herself saying, "By God, I'll see to it!"

Arriving at her destination, the beach, Amelia sighed and got out to stroll by the water's edge. Humming a Caribbean rhythm, her lean body glided along with the strolling tempo of the last sunny summer days. Her mood was melancholic. She dug her toes into the warmth of the wet mansion built among the rocks above, reaching out to the sea.

"Oh, my!" she gasped. Looking around, she noticed steps going upward toward the mansion. "I've got to try. See if anyone is there!" she thought. "Perhaps I'll find my way!"

Unlocked Doors

Observing a smooth stone path leading up to the mansion, she began the gentle climb. Barefoot yet pleased, the path was not difficult. Approaching the massive cyprus wood door, she noticed how it swung open with ease as if expecting a visitor.

Stepping inside, Amelia gasped as she drew in a big breath. Beyond the glass walls was the crystal blue sea, with billowing white clouds in the horizon, framing the green mountains beyond. What a view. Captivating! Her glance then looked at the vast white walls, adorned in black and white photographs, with one very huge oil painting on one wall. There was also a sculpture of a nymph grasping a fountain of flowing water and pointing to the spiral staircase that rose to the next floor above. Amelia felt light and graceful moving among all this beauty barefoot on the surface of cool onyx floors.

She was also exhausted, and the white sofa appealed to her body as she sank into it. Feeling safe, she thought of "The Three Bears" story. Giving up, Amelia's eyelids closed as she gratefully sank into a deep sleep.

Amelia awoke much later feeling rested but very hungry. Looking around, she found the kitchen and a bedroom nearby to investigate as soon as she found something to eat. The refrigerator was full which delighted and surprised her. Fixing an easy sandwich with a glass of milk, she went to the sand and noticed a breeze picking up, cooling her skin. Soon, it turned into wind as the sand blew, stinging her legs.

Looking down to brush away the clinging sand, she never saw the huge wave come up from the depth engulfing, dragging her into deep waters. Completely enveloped, she thought, "I am powerless to struggle, but I must breathe."

Her long blonde hair fanned out as she frantically looked to see the light above. Kicking with all her might, she swam toward it, breaking the surface of the water with a gasp for that first big breath. Amelia glanced around quickly over the water, looking for land or a boat. She spotted shadows coming toward her from a distance.

"Were it sharks or dolphins?" she wondered. Relief came over her when she saw the up and under movement of dolphins swimming. Coming alongside her, she reached out and grabbed a fin to hold on. She worked with their rhythm of dunking up and under until they turned to go further out to the sea. She saw an island and let go. Further away than anticipated, she lay on her back to float for a while. Her legs, back and arms felt tired and weak.

"It seems close, but how can she make it?" she wondered. Pondering and murmuring over her problem, she was lifted up and toward the island and tossed on the shore by a big swell of water.

Lying on the shore with the warmth of the sun restoring her energy, she gained back some strength. She knew she had the perseverance to survive to make the best of one's destiny, so she then hoisted herself up on her knees. When she looked herself over, she noticed her tattered halter and shorts.

Amelia knew she must venture forward as she got up. That's when she saw it! A white

Introduction

It was one of those nostalgic days as Amelia wanted to think back on all the joys and mistakes she had made to be able to look forward again. She knew it was necessary to learn from life with an honest review that may be hurtful. At this age of nineteen, there are choices to make, like crossing over lines that molds into more maturity, shaking off fear. This had to be done alone. She realized what was passed down while driving the car and thought of what her aunt had told about her mother, Marie. It seems that her mom was a young teenage lady when a Hollywood crew came to Amity to check out locations for a movie. While in town, they noticed mom shopping. Approaching her, they were polite and inquired if she had ever acted.

"No," she replied.

They asked, "Could we visit the parents to speak to them?"

Gleefully, she said, "Well, yes!"

When mom's parents, grandma and grandpa, heard their proposal, they refused. The director left, and Marie pitched a fit and had to be confined to her room to calm down. She never forgot her disappointment her entire life. Hence there was always, her daughter. Marie could see how she was developing into a pretty, personable child and envisioned her growing up into a beautiful young woman. Amelia was growing tall with long legs like her Dad. Her big blue eyes, blonde hair and winning smile, her own. Marie would pave the way for her to have the opportunities Marie did not have. She smiled to herself saying, "By god, I'll see to it!"

Arriving at her destination, the beach, Amelia sighed and got out to stroll by the water's edge. Humming a Caribbean rhythm her lean body glided along with the strolling tempo of the last sunny summer days. Her mood was melancholic. She dug her toes into the warmth of the wet become Wisdom. We will always work together," he related.

Amelia was enthralled never having thoughts of life this way.

"Come, let's get breakfast before our journey. I cook." He grinned.

The delicious breakfast of bacon, eggs, and toast supplied energy right down to her toes as she cleaned up the dishes and hummed a tune.

"Now," said Knowledge, "go to each gemstone doorknob and open the door to the room that will spell out your destiny of adventure. I will be with you."

Going to the screen, she asked, "How do I transfer all the learning of truth to my children?"

"Woman, you will take many years to experience the good and bad of life. No one is wise except for the One who was guided by the Creator of all. We have a guide—intuition, but most ignore it. Your children will learn, but in their own way. You will teach love. It is what is needed."

There was a sigh from Amelia. "Oh, I wish they didn't have to experience disappointment and pain."

Knowledge spoke, "Know you are emotionally speaking from a protective heart. Think of all you have learned. How else can goodness, happiness, and joy be expressed except by differences? They will learn that choice has consequences."

Acceptance came realizing she couldn't attain all the knowledge she yearned for. She inquired, "May I return here?"

Knowledge replied, "The door is always unlocked."

An Omen

Closing the heavy oak door behind them, she and Knowledge left to go to the rose quarts doorknob and enter this room to discover more. The room was smaller than the last and had three walls—one in black patent, one side in white silk, and the third in Pink ribbon-like walls. Directly ahead was a large wall of the window displaying the beautiful sea and billowing white clouds. Amelia spotted a comfortable white chair that she could certainly rest in and walked toward it. Noticing a book on the table, she reached for it. Its cover was white on one side and black on the other. Grasping the book, she sat on the sofa and she thought "Oh, my. How lovely."

Knowledge then settled in as Amelia proceeded to read.

Imagining a vision of angels busy, so busy plumping white clouds floating against a brilliant azure sky. This pure scene would soon be disrupted by ominous black clouds rolling in from the horizon. Mounds of gray-black swirls sulked from afar and approached rapidly toward the town of Amity. The advance seemed slow, but they moved in with purpose.

Jeff anxiously but carefully helped his pregnant wife, Marie, into the passenger's seat of their car when her hand gripped his arm with the strength of a wind-whipped gnarled branch.

"O-o-oh," she moaned softly, as another labor pain commanded her with tension.

This soon to be Madonna glanced at her husband's face while he assured her. "Don't worry, honey. I'll get you there in plenty of time."

The trust that filled her was a comfort. Jeff was a happy and proud man. He knew his polished Ebony 1935 Chevrolet with whitewall as his chariot, wheels that wouldn't let them down. He drove steadily, all the while thinking, "My nerves are shattered, but I can't let my weakness show!"

Marie glanced out the curved front window and noticed the ominous summer storm approaching. Finally arriving at the hospital, a friendly orderly assisted Marie into a wheelchair. Transitioning brought strain and again another labor pain of intensity came. Grasping at her husband's arm, announcing softly, "I do believe this baby of ours is in a hurry to see the world!"

Marie's labor contractions increased in frequency. The young frightened woman was whisked into the delivery room. Time was of the essence! As she lay on the cold stainless delivery table, timing her contractions, strong roars of thunder and flashes of lightning were notable.

The story of Amelia's birth was to be told over and over again to family and friends, and anyone else who fell under its spell. The battling conflict between luminosity and darkness on the day of this birth became an omen which would direct the child's life until her essence left this earth. In this small town, church chimes rang a melody at six o'clock along with a bell that tolled at that same hour every day. This birthing evening, as the chimes stopped at six o'clock, lightning struck a cruel bolt that sent heavenly light, shattering the sanctity of the birthing room. Then blackness, total blackness.

An old generator went to work and provided intermittent light with a cacophony of sighs and stutters defined the efforts. In the dancing light, Marie gave a final determined push. The doctor cried out, "She's here! Born between moments of light and dark! Dissension will always be with her under this sign."

As the doctor handed the little one over, he said, "Perfect. She is perfect."

Marie sighed. "Our Amelia is finally here." Then drifted off into a welcomed slumber.

The sky was silent once again. Its mission finished.

Amelia and Knowledge waited a few minutes, then got up to quietly leave.

Going to Town

"Here's the pearl doorknob." Knowledge remarked, "Let's go for a stroll in here." The room was spread out like Amity, Amelia's hometown, with a viewing screen on a fruit stand.

"It was amazing!" she thought, anxious to press the screen's button. Here we go!

Marie's morning chores were done. She sighed as she removed her headscarf, noticing the sunshine peeking through the lace curtains. It was a welcome to go outside this beautiful morning and breathe in the fragrant fresh spring air. Amelia was awakened from her nap. Marie dashed to the baby's bureau, taking out the prettiest pink blanket, then went back to wrap Amelia in it. Now they were ready to go as Amelia smiled at her Mom and let out a happy gasp. The stroller, in its newness, was easy to push. Noticing Amelia's big blue eyes gazing at everything she could, Marie was very happy. It was a short walk, but Marie was anxious to introduce her.

Arriving in town, Mrs. Smith was the first person encountered. "Oh, hello, Marie. Is this the new little one who's come to join the family?"

"Yes, this is our Amelia. She has become a delight to us."

"I can see that the little one is very pretty and sweet so just enjoy! It's good to see you in town, Marie."

"Thank you."

"Bye-bye," they both said.

Pushing on, Mr. Brown came out of his men's clothing store to see Amelia. "Ho, ho. What do we have here?" he bellowed. "A little beauty she is. Enjoy. I hope you'll all be happy."

"Thank you, Mr. Brown," replied Marie, as she moved forward.

Another visitor came down a step from his homemade ice cream shop. Mr. Peoples inquired, "What do we have here? My, a little beauty. Ah, yes, as soon as she can have my homemade ice cream, it's on me!" He grinned and then walked back in to his customers. "My," Marie thought, "his shop is always busy."

The "oh's and ah's" made Marie's heart soar with joy and pride. It then became a routine to walk to town most good days.

As Amelia grew, she continued to receive a warm reception from the townsfolk, and Amelia was beginning to walk and run. She preferred running. On these good days, Amelia either rode in a stroller or helped push it or hold her Mother's hand.

One day she let go to run out into the street. Suddenly Marie let out a scream and fainted. The car, moving slowly, stopped just in time. As the driver got out, Amelia was retrieved. Frightened, she was crying for her mommy to wake up. It wasn't long before she did as a gentleman assisted her to her feet. A small crowd began to form as the shop owner came outside.

Everything averted this almost disaster. Marie spread open her arms to hug her little girl. Everyone applauded. All was well.

Mr. Peoples brought out coffee for mom, settling her into a seat by the sidewalk and proceeded to give Amelia her first taste of vanilla ice cream. "Yummy!"

Everything turned out well. Marie finally smiled and thanked everyone. Picking up her little girl and placing her in her stroller, she walked home.

Thinking back on all that had just transpired, she thought, "The light has prevailed."

Knowledge reached over to turn off the video and said, "This is only the beginning. Time to go."

Following him out the door, Amelia could never imagine what was next.

Priming the Pump

Her eyes opened wide. As she saw this door, she gasped. "Looked at that doorknob. It has a ruby in its center."

"All is not as it seems. It's genuine. Let's go in," spoke Knowledge.

The door again was unlocked and opened to a view Amelia didn't expect. It was the interior of her home. Her bedroom and the living room were displayed, exactly.

"What?" she thought.

They sat to listen to the story on an old phonograph on an end table, about how Amelia came to wear curls. You may not understand it. Her mother did when her baby reached four years old. She became a project: a Shirley Temple look-alike.

Amelia was seated on a stool and wiggled. A bop on the head brought her to attention. It was the most uncomfortable process. Amelia's Mother tore up old sheets and rags and the end placed on top of her head.

"Hold this," her mother called out.

"Ouch!" Amelia gasped while her Mom wrapped her damp hair around the sheet strip and tied it on top. It seemed as ridiculous as it was uncomfortable, especially with her brother making fun of her. Her mother spoke to him saying, "If you continue to make fun, I will put your hair in curls too!" With that comment, he ran out of the room and never said another word.

In the mornings, there were curls galore—brushing them over her finger until they bounced all over her head with one special curl on top of her head for the ribbon bow that matched her outfit. Her head bobbed its way to breakfast while Marie planned a trip to town. She was always delighted to go to town, especially for the ice cream from Mr. Peoples. The other shop owners always say "hello," waving us by with a smile. If she ever resisted going, she'd feel a pinch on her arm.

Phase two:

Christmas was approaching this "Year of the Curls," and Marie had volunteered her daughter to stand up on stage for the Christmas pageant and sing "Jingle Bells." Things were moving forward. With enough pinches, Amelia's dress of red gauze with silver bells was ready too.

She was told to shake while she sang and move around to ring the bells, and when she did, her curls bounced too. Everyone laughed. She searched for her mom who waved and smiled, so she guessed everything was alright.

Curl episodes went on with no end in sight. Talking or crying did not work. Trying to sleep was to no avail as the rags hurt her head.

"Please, Mom! It hurts and it's hard to sleep. Please take them out!"

"Not yet," she replied, vehemently.

Amelia wondered what to do. One cleaning day, she was in the living room straightening things when she moved her grandmother's sewing kit. Noticing a pair of scissors there, she took them out. Her mother went out to the grocery store, so she hid behind the sofa and "wack," went the top curl. She cut off two more in front when she heard her mom's car returning from shopping.

She crouched in as deeply into the seat as she could in fear. Her mom came in and shrieked,

"What have you done?"

Her grandmother came rushing from the kitchen and saw in a flash what was happening. She was grabbed out of her seat and given the hardest spanking ever!

"Stop!" her grandmother called, reaching for Amelia and giving her a hug.

"I think it's time to stop this," she said.

"I think you may be right," said her mom.

That night, her hair was for the first time in what seemed forever, brushed out. She felt normal now and alright to go to school.

Knowledge quipped, "First spanking, huh? Was it worth it?" he asked.

"You bet!" was the answer.

The best and happiest adventure for Amelia became school. She began the habit of staying as long as she could because she liked the teachers and other students. Later in high school, her favorite course was chemistry, and besides sports, her ideal adventure was being the lead in the senior play. But Knowledge shared, "Don't want to jump ahead, as there are a lot more doors to open."

"So, let's go!" Amelia exclaimed.

Knowledge then gently took her hand and said, "This was not a door I wanted you to enter, but it tells a lot so stay with me," he explained.

She stepped beside him closer and proceeded to reach the black opal door knob.

Innocence

The black onyx doorknob was a simple and smooth design. It shone in the sunlight as Amelia reached out to open the unlocked door to a wooded wonderland.

As a little girl, Amelia believed in fairies. Oh, she definitely did believe! Her tiny creatures with gossamer wings and sparkling gowns lived in the woods, creating cozy cottages in tree stumps, banks of leaves and even on lily pads floating in secret lakes. As the fairies' interests flitted, the creatures delicately found their fun alighting on flowers and feathery ferns.

Each day when she walked home from school, Amelia chose to take a long way home, one that took her through the deepest, darkest woods. Cemetery stones were scattered in her forest. Had this been a church cemetery a hundred years before? Amelia sauntered through the woods for months before she recognized what the mossy tablets might be as Mother Nature had claimed them and covered the etched stones with blankets of green. She tried to read the names on the markers, but the elements and years had made them all but disappeared.

Delicate Vinca Minor laid a carpet of purple under massive oaks and begged to be picked. A burst of yellow wood daisies surprised the field of lavender and created a puzzle of blooms.

Amelia imagined clusters of fairies were watching as she made her way home. Feeling guilty at times, she would whisper, "You know, it's perfectly fine for me to pick the prettiest flowers to give to the neighbors who can't get out. I just want to see them smile."

Smiles beamed on Amelia when she brought bouquets of periwinkles to her shut-in friends; along with the smiles came pennies and dimes of gratitude that Amelia saved for ice cream treats. She always remembered to favor her fairies on her way home from the confectionary shop. Taking bits of her sugar cone, Amelia placed them in a fairy maze on mounds of moss. She prayed for the protection of her little friends and knew the missing bits of the ice cream cone meant her tiny pixies were well fed by her offering.

Arriving home from school one late spring day, Amelia heard her mother speaking on the phone.

"Why, hello, Betty. How nice you are visiting the neighborhood. I'll bring Amelia, and we'll drive up to see you."

Amelia changed from school clothes, a khaki skirt and patterned blouse, to a pretty yellow and pink flowered dress. Her mom wrapped a loaf of banana bread she had baked that morning to gift her friend, and soon the mother and daughter took the short drive to north Amity. The welcome was warm and friendly as the old friends began to catch up.

Noticing Amelia was left out of the conversation, Betty offered, "There's a girl about your age who lives three doors down. Why don't you run over and see if she can play?"

Happy to escape the dull adult conversation, Amelia skipped to the house thinking she'd find a new friend. Several knocks on the door went unanswered, but finally, a muscular, unkempt man opened the heavy door and simply stared at the young girl who had disturbed his afternoon nap.

"Is Suzy home?" Amelia asked timidly. "Come in," welcomed the man. "Suzy is shopping with her mom but will be back very soon. Why don't you come in and wait for her?"

Before she could reply, he roughly took Amelia's hand and sat down on the sagging couch, dragging her firmly towards him.

He exclaimed, "My, what a pretty little girl you are and wearing such a pretty dress too!" The man grabbed the hem of her dress and pulled it up to expose Amelia's pink panties. She tried to push her dress down, but the man held both her wrists with one gnarled hand. Amelia's heart began to race as fear took hold. She was afraid to scream as his finger groped hungrily under her panties.

As Amelia tried to escape the man's persistent probing, her mind floated to her forest fairies. The presence of such delicate creatures seemed to soothe the pain she was feeling. The fairies were circling her, offering protection and a message of strength and love! Amelia then knew she would be okay, but it was up to her to take a stand.

The man smelled funny, and Amelia knew he was the bad man adults warned kids to avoid. His assault was rough and frightening. Carrying the fairies' message close to her heart, she had to fight back! Amelia pulled away and stood up quickly, back to the front door. Suddenly standing, the man rushed to the bathroom, and his groans were heard bleating from behind the closed door.

Terrified, Amelia found her voice and timidly asked, "Can I go now?"

A muffled "yes" came from the bathroom.

Amelia ran back to Miss Betty's house as fast as she could, remembering what the man had warned as she fumbled to unlock the door that had held her prisoner. "Don't you dare tell anyone, or I'll find you and hurt you!"

Walking into the room, her mom casually commented, "You sure weren't gone very long."

Amelia simply said, "Suzy wasn't home."

Amelia sat still and quiet in a chintz chair as Betty and her mother continued their conversation. Holding a plate of sugar cookies Betty had generously offered, Amelia could only stare at the floor, too frightened to move.

She held back tears as she wondered, *why would anyone try to hurt me?*

That was the day Amelia knew exactly why she would never talk to strangers. A valuable but frightening lesson to learn. She also learned her fairies were real and would forever be guiding and protecting her, her whole life long.

She took her shame to heart as she tried to forget her secret. Knowledge sat beside her and with sympathy said, "Remember it's not your fault!"

She looked at him, weakly smiled, and said, "Let's get out of here!"

A Time to Cry

a.e.ames

A young girl's feet
went many place
others wouldn't go.

Walked to school
by a cemetery, where
flowers grew in spring.

Picked pretty posies
sold to local ladies
pennies bought ice cream.

Walking warm days by the
woods gave a place for
sunshine, filtering in.

A moss carpet stirred her mind.
smooth stones made a fence,
as night fairies, ate crumbs.

Beauty she saw everywhere,
sharing her winning smile
then came, a time to cry.

Most of all drifting in the breezes along Great South Bay. It was next summer she was hired by the Forest family to babysit their children at the Yacht Club—a fun way to earn money for mom and save some for school clothes.

Graduation from Amity High at seventeen required fifteen accredited points in order to leave. Having earned them six months before graduation, the school gave Amelia permission to work.

Reading the newspaper want ads, she found that a dentist was moving to a town nearby and was wanting to train an assistant. Applying with the Forrest's recommendation, she acquired the job. Excited, she arrived with a notebook in hand, ready to learn and work.

Knowledge took a deep breath and cringed, "There is much yet ahead to learn, and it's not all good." With a frown, Amelia glanced at him furrowing her forehead.

The job seemed interesting, and she passed a tooth extraction with flying colors. It did not bother her so the dentist said, "You are ready to learn to read X-rays." Guiding her into the darkroom, he turned out the lights. All was expected except when he stood behind her: leaning in, grabbing her breasts, attempting to kiss her neck. She was so startled she flew back in astonishment, out the door, grabbing her purse, down the steps, jumping into her car and trembled so much she had to take some time to calm down. She finally did and drove toward home. She'd never return, not even for her paycheck hoping he'd have the decency to mail it.

He did not. Just how to tell Mom about this was a problem? She didn't want to upset her. Stopping at the red light, waiting for it to change, she noticed a "Help Wanted" sign in an Arthur Murray studio across the street. Pulling up, she went inside to inquire. As she spoke, the lovely lady listened intently, interviewed her, she was hired. She would be initially trained for a full week then put on commission selling lessons and teaching.

Going home, telling mom about her new choice would make her pleased. She knew dancing was a joy as was teaching. She seemed to fit right in with her new friends. Getting ready to do demonstrations was a highlight. The dance partner and Amelia soon developed a crush on each other and one day, he invited her on a date.

He said, "I have to sell my motorcycle and buy a car, so I can't pick you up until Saturday evening."

I replied, "The telephone will ring with your call. I'm patient."

He smiled and then left.

I told mom, mentioning dancing with him, and telling the nostalgic look in her eyes she was thinking of dad. I got busy Saturday, picked out clothes having them ready and was happy. It didn't last. The phone rang, and picking it up, I was startled as the woman was crying.

"Is this Amelia?" she asked

"Yes," hesitating in reply. More tears then.

"Bret was killed earlier driving his bike home after it was sold," she gasped. "A driver drove through a stop sign and wasn't even hurt, but the impact flew Bret off his vehicle. He had told me about you. Darlin', I am sorry my heart is broken for my son."

She hung up without another word as I stood still holding the phone.

I couldn't dance anymore for a while, and it was alright financially. I was working for the Forest's children, and they paid very well. Dr. Forest gave me some office work and feeling appreciated felt nice.

It was time to return to school for graduation preparation. The English teacher approached in the hall saying, "There's a senior play I wish you'd try out for."

I asked, "Will I have ample time?"

"Of course. We'll have enough time for the rehearsals. See you on Monday for tryouts".

Some of my friends tried out and was very surprised to be told I had the lead.

Wow! Showing up for the rehearsals, studying my part became full time. After a while, Ms. Olean took the co-lead aside to tell us to date some and hangout as the end of the play we had to kiss. She felt we ought to get to know each other better. We did go out over to the infamous OBI with many of his friends. So much fun! The night of the play, our kiss got known all over the school. Teasing took on a new meaning. The kiss was never forgotten!

College had to be put off until much later as my stepdad died suddenly after the play. Refusing the church for scholarship for missionary work, finding a good job was scheduled in for me.

Knowledge patted my hand. "You're learning."

Safe Places

Knowledge took her by the hand saying, "Are you ready to start? Here is where we first met." He stood before a large doorknob of golden topaz, reminding her to have courage and go inside. There standing before them were shelves of books and on a table was a television screen with a video of her old brick school in Amity. On a wall were photographs of her family, her school friends, her home, and even Ada on a beach day.

Looking around, Amelia saw everything was decorated minimal in beige and topaz linen. The sofa once again for comfort. Sitting near the screen, Amelia noticed a near button she pressed it. Hence, a story was revealed.

The streets were shaded by large oak trees growing on both sides of the street. There at the back of three large trees stood a red brick, two-story, rectangular school building.

It was the junior high school in Amelia's hometown. To her, it was her safe place. Entering these doors always put a smile on her face.

The classes were planned until three p.m. each weekday, after which brought extra-curricular activities and sports. She'd leave at five p.m. and stop at the homemade ice cream store for pound cake with a scoop of homemade ice cream and a coca-cola. Walking the mile home would work it off, and she maintained slimness. It wasn't given much thought back then. The world of learning in school brought friendship, and teachers smile especially when she did well in class. Coaches like her attitude in sports as she gave her best efforts. She was center position in basketball, played in hockey, volleyball, and ran track. She earned her school letter and no one knew she was the gossip editor of the high school "Echo" paper.

In junior high, few knew her best friend, Ada. She was pretty, smart, and from Denmark. She would work after school in her parents' delicatessen and occasionally invited me there. I learned to be helpful and would peel potatoes for salad or decorate platters for parties. Ada's mom often sent home delights for my mom and it was always a good time. Ada's parents worked on the weekends so we'd get together and study. We both love math and English with chemistry as Amelia's favorite. One day just before graduation from school, Ada announced, "We will be moving soon. The family will be far away, and we won't see each other again." She cried.

"Oh, no," I said, as we hugged. It was so sad for us and true.

"I have to give a speech at graduation," she told me. She did, and it was intelligent and lovely. After this, we hugged and cried, and I never see my friend again. Amelia's heart felt null and void with her best friend gone.

She opened the front door, and there was no "hello."

The furniture stood still as if waiting for attention. Opening the window for fresh air, Amelia felt no breeze. The only sounds were from the creaking steps as she went up the wooden steps to her lonely room. Her home was not a safe place in its emptiness. Her quest was not to be there and to keep busy elsewhere.

School clubs and sports were attainable as was her job babysitting for the Forests. She would also keep her home clean out of discipline and habit. She taught Sunday school and sang in the choir with her cousin. Then later, the minister asked, "Could you start a youth program for teens from school here on Sunday evenings?"

"I could try," she replied to the inquisitive look on his face.

"That would be excellent!" he joyfully remarked with a smile.

So Amelia did. She was the president for four years, and it was a nice success. One night in high school, there was another basketball game featuring my friends. Amelia was asked to hold some "lucky charms" for they thought it would bring them luck. Although they were really good, they gave credit to the charms. They were true friends and would come over often to eat at our table, and mom welcomed them with a big smile. Especially at Thanksgiving, they'd come for round two at our table. These basketball heroes heard that mom was going out of town for a week so they came over, dads in tow, and remodeled the kitchen and wallpapered and painted the living room.

When Marie returned, I thought she'd faint but gasped instead. "Oh, my!" she cried. "You all will be here for a celebration dinner. She clipped right out to the store and did exactly that. A good time was enjoyed by all.

A new boy arrived from out of town to our school. Attempting the basketball team, he noticed me and invited me to a movie. He seemed polite and with a nice manner, so I agreed. He seemed nervous walking home, and when arriving there, he bent down for a kiss which was refused. Pulling back in a huff, he stalked off!

Opening the door, I thought, "That didn't go very well." His ego must have been hurt so bad that at basketball practice that Monday, he told his friends what an "easy" mark Amelia was. Without any more provocation, the guys simply bounced on him and beat him up as the story goes. Even the coach didn't report it. My heroes!

The Skiff Meets the Sea

Amelia was so proud that she owned such a fine little craft that perhaps asking that anyone who wanted to sail could help her sand, calk and paint the boat with her each spring. That idea came from reading Huckleberry Finn and some of his ideas made sense. Not many offers came through, so sailing often was her private world.

Sailing many days that summer, she often thought of her grandpa and his twinkling blue eyes that always seemed to hold a private story—sending him thoughts of thanks for the time and effort he made on the sailboat. She felt it was a labor of love.

As she left the dock, she pushed the centerboard down halfway and unfurled the sail, catching the breeze. Grasping the tiller with one hand and gripping the sheet rope with the other, off she went with the wind circumnavigating the vast bay. The landlocked world left behind was no longer important. The princess of the waves was on her way.

The water tapped a song on the sides of the boat beginning a rhythm for a tune. Amelia was lulled into realizing this perfect day was properly her last likelihood of freedom, as she looked toward the horizon seeing that that the main channel was only a short distance away. Amelia's mom had warned her to stay away from the South Bay channel because it was a route for the large yachts to venture to the ocean. She could be swamped in their traverse trips or be forced to sail out further than intended. The big bad Atlantic Ocean was the end of the channel and in its business would be too big a challenge for a small craft. Sailing and boating so often had developed trust on the waters and offered our family companionship. Having lulled into daydreaming suddenly, like siren's song, the gateway to the Atlantic beaches beckoned. Putting aside any worries she had as she visualized, maneuvering her boat along the busy beaches, crowded with tan bodies, her mom's voice planted an earworm in her psyche, but she argued that a short adventure into the channel would not cause harm so she grabbed the opportunity to explore.

"Yipes, better hurry," she thought, as white fluffy clouds began to grow and pucker with puffs of gray when the sun played peekaboo. Knowing that summer storms don't usually arrive until late afternoon, she wasn't too concerned. This fine day time wasn't of the essence.

As Amelia sailed into the channel entrance, there was a sudden "boom," and the sail lunged across her shoulders, the wind shifting dramatically. This was totally a sudden uncontrolled jibe! As quickly as it changed direction, it stopped, stopped dead in its tracks. Tacking in an effort to find puffs to fill the sail, she maneuvered along the reed line of the marshes. The boat and time moved slowly.

Amelia began to doubt the wisdom of her decision, venturing into uncharted waters. The realization hit her hard that with no wind, it could take her hours to paddle with attempts to sail back to the docks.

The wind being becalmed had no sound, so all she heard was the rumble in her stomach. Vague feelings of uneasiness began nagging at her and feelings of hunger quickly left her thoughts.

Realizing she did have a tool to use, she reached and twisted the oar out from under the seat perch and was soon paddling one side then across to the other, not making much headway. Her arms began to ache, and she made herself a promise to have a sailboat one day with an engine to be able to handle anything that Mother Nature threw her way.

Her fantasies disappeared when suddenly she became aware of an alarming change around her. The quiet water world around her that was calm resounded with a roar of marine engines heading straight for her boat. Glancing around, completely surprised and shocked into panic, the yachts were full throttled down the channel to reach the safety of land.

Gasping at the magnitude of what she saw, she couldn't think, much less respond! Boat wakes tossed her boat as an apple on All Hollows' Eve. Rough waters pushed her further toward where she had been told never to go. Black clouds loomed on the horizon, tumbling over each other in a frenzied roll. The inflated wind pulled at her rig as she flew forward, almost capsizing. The oar was pulled out of her hands. She had to let go.

Releasing the sheet rope as she frantically hung on, it pulled her almost overboard as she futilely tried to control the winds' force. The boat was lifted higher and higher as it moved faster and faster forward toward the beach. As the beachside dock loomed in front, she would be driven into it. Ocean waves were coming faster and more forceful, rendering her helpless using the tiller or rudder. Amelia became nothing as the force of the wind and sea took over. She tried calling above the winds' roar, but she was a whisper in the water wilderness.

Alone by the lean-stand, her fatigued body fought the cold brought on by the pelting rain as she began to ache and hurt. As the storm was quieting down, she wept then fell asleep in the corner of the stand.

It seemed like days, not hours, had passed when she heard a voice calling. Was she in heaven? As the sounds grew closer and louder, she attempted to stand but to no avail. Hope was stirring in her veins as well as energy called upon, as she spied a jeep crawling, slogging passed the heavy thick sand. The young men in the jeep kept calling out her name.

"Here I am!" Amelia called out, attempting to stand as she struggled to be upright. Her legs were heavy, unmovable, and weak. She couldn't make them work no matter what she tried, massaging her calves in cadence with cries of pain.

The jeep passed, her spirit fell and then rose again when the driver did a double back, closer to her hiding place. Amelia called out as loud as she could until the young men finally found her. They were grinning as she cried. A man wrapped her in a warm blanket while the other called home and informed that she had been found, alive.

As they tried to calm and distract her, she was told how someone from a yacht had called the Coast Guard of seeing a young gal in a small sailboat caught out in the storm. It had been a hurricane, unexpected, that hit suddenly. Mom had made frantic calls to anyone who would listen and begged authorities to keep searching, saying that "although young, she is a good sailor."

Thank goodness I was at last headed home. They pulled up to the house. The family rushed out to greet her, not sure if it was her or her ghost. Mom and Amelia collided in a hug that lasted for a very long time.

Later, it was time for "the talk." Her mom told her she had suffered enough by the experience and in losing her, valued sailboat. She had surrendered her boat of happiness to Davy Jones' Locker.

When Amelia remembers that day, tears still well up in her eyes. The experience of loss of control, safety, and finally, the loss of her boat is overwhelming. She never did get that boat. It was a lesson learned, and then some.

Contests

My friend Knowledge said, "No time to relax," as he gripped the opal doorknob. It swung open, revealing two sections. One side was an ocean beach with a boardwalk and the other, a movie theater lobby.

"How strange," Amelia thought.

"Not so," murmured Knowledge. "Let's go to the movie theatre first."

She followed, and the people there were casting votes toward the photographs on the standing board. She saw hers then gasped in surprise. Looking over her shoulder, she saw a movie reel telling the story of tulip festival time.

In a town named Babylon on Long Island, New York off Merrick Road stands a hand-built replica of a windmill, imported from Holland. Built and moved in the 1950s, the Babylon township decided to celebrate sponsoring a tulip festival. This parade would represent the local town and would conclude at the windmill location.

Everyone who was on board and happy with this idea decided to have floats representing each town, with a local "princess" riding on it. She would be chosen by the local residents in a voting method. Brother Jim took his sister's photo to the manager of the theater, placing her in the running. There was a slot under the photo for votes.

Amelia hesitated to attend the movies, embarrassed. The Manager called one day to explain, "the voting was going very good, and that Amelia would be appearing before the Judges and would need a grown. They would also ask a few questions."

Mrs. Forest went along with her and her mom to select the gown. Amelia wanted her input as she enjoyed her taste in clothes. They found the perfect gown, one she could also wear to the prom. Five of us were then selected to go up on the stage, walk across, and then answer the questions given by the judges. Her knees felt like they would buckle, but some of the shyness left as she wasn't as nervous as she thought. The gentleman judge came over to her handling the microphone then all was silent as the judges conferred. It was time for the call-out of winners and the second runner-up was called, and it wasn't her. Then the first runner up, it was who I thought, had it sewed up. The dealership dame didn't take it very well from the scowl on her face. Then the winner! Nerves were at a crunch as a judge came forward taking Amelia by the hand, escorting her up to the mic and exploding the words, "Your Winner, Miss Amity, Amelia Nyquist!"

All hell broke loose in the audience. My brother and his friends whistled and stomped, my family and friends cried out, and the applause was deafening. Mayhem cut loose. Her nerves sprung loose, and she cried tears of surprise and joy. As we were preparing to leave, the manager congratulated us on behalf of the town, and we went home with our group to the party.

Mom had splurged on a bottle of champagne, and brother opened it, handing me a glass of my first to enjoy. Mother also handed me an envelope that the manager handed her for me. It was filled with gift certificates from the merchants in the village.

"Wow!" I thought, hardly believing this was all happening.

Amelia was still "heady" the next morning. Like in a dream, she awoke, staring at the large white envelope. She went down to breakfast and heard her mom singing in the kitchen. They immediately went walking to visit the merchants. They were very delighted and generous with their gifts. Mom opened the dining room table to display all the gifts. It was mind-boggling!

The parade date was creeping up, and Amelia had decided who would ride in the yellow Buick convertible. Amelia was sixteen, and her little friend Pippa would ride next to her adorned in a Dutch costume. My brother drove, and my cousin Mitch is in the passenger's seat as Pippa's escort. The folks waved and smiled as we did too, and it was all shared happiness with a tinge of pride. What a glorious day!

Knowledge suggested they sit awhile to relax. Before long, Amelia was anxious to proceed, so they moved over to the beachside. Somehow, Amelia's attire changed into a swimsuit. She was walking on a boardwalk. The nearby sign was displaying a video.

New York Model

It was one of those clear, sunny lazy days of a Long Island summer when Marie walked into her daughter's room to say, "Let's go to Jones Beach!"

This announcement caused Amelia to sit up straight from bed, replying, "Mom, are you OK? You don't like the beach."

"Well, honey, it's such a pretty day. It will be lovely to walk to the boardwalk and talk about your future."

Amelia loved the beach, so she readily agreed before her mom changes her mind. It took them only minutes to get ready. Donning swimsuits, cover-ups, and sunhats and tossing lotion in the bag, off they went. Amelia munched on a muffin she grabbed going out the door. Her mother was actually smiling as she placed a basket in the back seat.

On a Tuesday, the traffic was light, parking easy, as the good day began. Amelia breathed in a sigh of happiness as she breathed in the ocean's fragrance and saw the waves breaking along the sdhore. The vivid blue sky had the company of a few white clouds floating along the horizon. A-a-ah, perfection!

As they strolled along the boardwalk searching for the right spot to settle, Amelia noticed three people, not in bathing suits, but in casual wear coming toward them. One man was carrying a camera, the other a case, and the woman approached mom and said, "We are from Newsday and are conducting a search for a model. It's a contest that will run over the next month, and photographs will be printed in the newspaper until five gals are selected. Then they will be selected to go to the "Stork Club for lunch for one to be chosen for the Conover Model Agency in New York. May we photograph your daughter?"

It was at that moment she understood why her mother took her to the beach. She felt weak but replied, "Its OK, Mom."

There are some things Amelia could not confront or understand. They did not stay long that day as her mom's mission was accomplished. They found a spot near the ocean and sat on their blanket to eat the picnic lunch. After eating the fruits in the basket, Amelia took a dip in the ocean, and they left. Although her mom seemed happy, there was little conversation driving home.

The time sitting for the Forest children and watching for the Newsday photos all went by quickly. One day as she got home just before dinner, her mom showed her a note written with a phone message saying, "Honey, you are one of the five selected by the agency! Candy Jones called earlier with the invitation to lunch at the Stork Club in two weeks!"

Amelia and her mom hugged as her mother's happiness she couldn't resist.

Marie shifted gears and got shopping for her daughter. She treated Amelia shopping at Sak's Fifth Avenue. She purchased: a new dress, high heels, and a manicure. She felt so very pampered. The plan was that Marie would drive Amelia into the city to the Stork Club, drop her there, and later pick her up. Marie knew to spend her time window shopping.

The day arrived driving up to the doorman who was dressed in a red coat with decorations on it that glittered in the sun. He handsomely opened her door, as well as the restaurant's door and made her feel very important. Drawing her shoulder up and back, she planned to act as regal as this teen could. Greeted by Candy Jones, introductions were made as she was shown a seat at an elegantly adorned table. Everything was so fine, especially the dessert. An ice cream scoop of vanilla with shredded coconut sprinkled on it topped with a drizzle of hot fudge. It was called "snowball." Ms. Jones sat at every table, conversing with each contestant. She was an attractive, interesting lady as she inquired about each of us. Leaving, we were told they'd be in touch in a few days. Amelia thanked them for a lovely luncheon and left, with her mom waiting at the curb. The adventure was shared in detail to her captive audience on the way home.

Three days went by slowly until the phone rang. The call was from Ms. Jones telling us that Amelia was selected as the winner of the contest. She went off to work at the Yacht Club while back at home, Marie called her family and prepared a small surprise party. The whole bit of balloons and cake were served as Marie sported an attitude of "my daughter, the New York model!"

Scheduling a trip by train was not difficult as it took an hour to arrive at Penn station and plenty.

California on Call

Carl was Amelia's bachelor godfather who took care of his ill mother until she died two years after dad. We were all good friends. After the deaths of our beloved family members, Carl took mother out. They were dating, and it couldn't be happier. He was a patient, kind and hardworking man who enjoyed mom and Amelia. Their special time was on Sunday nights going to the movies, then buying ice cream cones on the way home. Other times, mom invited him over for supper.

Nearing her sixteenth birthday, Amelia was asked what she wanted for her birthday. Amelia spoke up, "I would like something very special, but it depends on you! I would like for you and Carl to marry so we could be a family."

Mother cried and gave a big hug around my neck. "Well, we'll see," she said.

My girlfriend's date could drive, so we set up a plan around that. We all met at this fancy French restaurant near town. There was a note on the table as we approached. It read, "My Darling, Carl and I are driving to New England to get married on this special birthday of yours. You have made it very special for us too! You are loved, Honey! Happy birthday!"

The dinner was heavenly and the dessert my favorite, Coconut layer cake! Wow! What a fabulous birthday.

The day after the best birthday ever, making pancakes in the kitchen, flipping them as my uncle showed us, they would be delicious! The phone rang, upsetting my focus. An efficient, official voice spoke, "Asking please for a Mrs. Nyquist."

Telling the lady she was away for her honeymoon, she said, "This is urgent." Continuing on, she said, "It must be your uncle that died suddenly before surgery yesterday. He is to have an official burial at sea, and we need your mother to fly out here in California and sign the papers."

"I have to wait until she calls me."

She replied, "Alright, please make it as soon as you can."

Saying that this is not impossible, she'd be phoned.

Mother called two days after, and the story of her brother was revealed. She came home with Carl the next day. It only took her a day or so to call California and fly out there. Carl was nice to have around. He was jolly and joked a lot.

Mother's brother was a chef in the Merchant Marines. In peacetime, he had his own restaurant in California. He would tell us all about the movie stars that are there. After my dad died, uncle would come to visit us more often. He would take us out. Clothes shopping was Amelia's biggest thrill. He made me feel very grown up. At thirteen, he picked a lovely dress out for me. I didn't feel like a kid when my uncle was around. He played checkers with us and other card games. He was fun. These memories were happy, but now it is sad as his life was over, and he couldn't come see us again. Nor ever again! Crying for the loss of him, he became a nice memory.

Mother went to California alone by airplane and came back about seven days later. She drove back because of a yellow Buick convertible he left her. Wow, she looked good driving it!

Mom told us all about the memorial service they had on board the ship. Then too, the burial at sea. Mom said, "How nice it was and wished we could have been there."

Knowledge had to speak, "There is knowledge in all things. There is more to living and you must go to experience more of it."

"OK, here we go!" sang out Amelia.

Some of the Best

After the senior play, a memory was in her head of Ms. Oleans telling, "Her uncle observed the play and noticed Amelia as a model for his designs." She described his offices in New York City as a designer salon, and he sold beautiful gowns to Saks Fifth Ave. and Lord and Taylor. They were so majestic, often placed for design in the windows.

Going to the safe place to speak with Ms. Oleans about this, she phoned him.

Speaking to Amelia, he said, "Please come in Monday for interview."

Replying, "Yes, I will. Thank you for the opportunity."

"This would be an adventure!" speaking to myself.

Telling this to mom brought a smile, and she was happy with me. Monday came and taking the train into the city, an experience not to miss. Out on the street, the buildings were tall and stately as the crowd of people swarmed by. Few looked up or smiled. The office was in walking distance to Penn Station. Arriving there ready, greeted by Mr. Shea and his brother, the office manager, I was then introduced to Annie, the designer. She was nice and friendly.

Measuring me in the designing room, she reported this was a perfect size for the job position.

Told what my weekly salary would be, I left ready to start next week. Having been told once that, "Destiny directs our paths." It was believable right now. Catching the early train for home, I was anxious to share the news.

At last, there could be regular bill payments as soon as we could get into the drawer stuffed with bills. My head was filled with wonder of just how to approach this. Amelia had monthly train passes and walked home from the train station about seven p.m.

Still summer light shone in a sunset, and a gentle breeze stirred in the quiet. She stepped onto the porch, hearing the telephone. Answering it, she heard mom's voice wearily say, "I have bad news, Honey. Dad has had a heart attack and is in the intensive Care Unit."

"Be right there," she firmly stated. "Don't be frightened. He's in an oxygen tent and the doctor said Carl will be here for a while."

Leaving the house and driving as fast as she could, Amelia walked into Carl's room and stared at his withdrawn face. A chill ran through her. Mom came into the room and the nurse recommended that they both go down to the cafeteria for a bite. When they told Carl they would go just for a few minutes, he smiled. Other times during the month, he seemed too weak and slept most of the time.

It all occurred near their second anniversary and Amelia's eighteenth birthday. It was a month in which the doctor gave permission for dad to come home. Mom was to order a hospital bed. Friends came over to help her convert the dining room into a hospital room. There was also a bathroom downstairs near it. Dad soon arrived by ambulance home but was too weak to manage walking. He sat in a wheelchair and rolled in. We laughed with him.

I would be up early to take the train into the city and always go around and give a "good morning" kiss to dad. It was a silent, still sunny morning when I was entering in to see dad, I noticed that he suddenly sat up, raised out his hands, smiled in a broad grin as the lace curtains blew straight out. With a moan, he gently lay back lifeless. Transfixed, calling Mom, she came in from the kitchen and ... fainted. Reaching for the phone to call an ambulance and later, an undertaker cousin of ours was able to get mom on her feet into the kitchen for some water which shook as she drank it.

Three months went by in a more normal routine that seemed rote with no emergency or fun, nor extra money to use. About this time, the insurance man arrived to give my mother the deed to the house. It was a plan that Carl took out. Introduced to him, his name was Barry Adams, who wrote this type of insurance. He came in, I offered iced tea, and he noticed mom's reactions. She acted non-communicative and numb. I had noticed how, whenever bills arrived, she simply stored them in the large bureau in the dining room. The phone would constantly ring during the day and now in the evenings. They were will collectors. The phone rang when Barry was there, and it wasn't answered.

Barry said, "Don't you want to answer that?"

"No," mother stated. "It's only a bill collector!"

He looked surprised and looked at me. "Are you having trouble paying?" he asked.

Amelia answered, "I think so. Mother hides the bills."

"Where are they?" he asked.

Believing they were in the large bureau drawer, opening it up, we saw it was stashed with piles of unopened envelopes.

"Oh, my! "Amelia retorted.

Barry didn't flinch. He took his handkerchief though and wiped his brow. Embarrassed tears ran down Amelia's cheeks. Barry stood up, looking down into the drawer and said, "I'll make an appointment with my friend who is an excellent psychologist for your mother and come back next week and help you know something about this, and it will work." He added, "In the meantime, open and organize all of these papers, and I'll bring the rest with me."

Whew! I felt relief for mom and for me. I knew she needed some help too.

The following week, Barry showed up with notebooks, pencils, and envelopes. I had done the overwhelming job of opening and putting the bills in alphabet order. It was ready. Mom had started the therapy sessions, and it felt good as she seemed to be responding.

Amelia was shown how to add and divide the amounts into monthly payment according to her salary. She wrote a letter of agreement to them, saying this payment would arrive every month in a regular fashion. They agreed. For an extra payment, babysitting came up, and Dr. Forest had me doing some office paperwork. This income helped, learning the word and honor at least for Amelia.

Three weeks went by, and the routine was working, but there was no money left to spare for fun times. Mom talked to Amelia to tell her how much better she felt with her new job title in the school cafeteria and counseling. She added character to her white uniform by placing a colored handkerchief in the pocket to match her earrings. She was soon recommended to the agricultural college trained as a dietician. Very excited, it took two years. She was then hired in a prestigious home for the blind on the North Shore. Mom had pulled out and up just fine as Amelia was proud of her.

These few months had passed when Barry came back to check in. I hadn't called to tell him how good everything was going, so he pulled up the door one Saturday. He approached mother to ask, "I think Amelia has worked hard to get all this out of debt, and I honestly believe she needs a night out!"

Looking at Mom for an answer, she said, "It's up to Amelia."

She didn't know how to answer her mother, so Amelia replied, "I guess it's OK!"

Telling Annie at work about this older mentor asking her out, she seemed pleased. She asked, "Where are you going so we can shop for a dress!"

"A nice surprise!" Annie spoke. "Let's go to lunch and buy a little black dress!"

We found the perfect dress and lovely black strap shoes then went back to work. The following Saturday, Amelia was driven into New York to see a musical and go to dinner.

We dined at the Vesuvio Restaurant. The food was superior, but the coffee cups were tiny. Barry and Amelia talked while the coffee cups kept being refilled. Mr. Vesuvio came up later to the table and said, "I have never had anyone consume as much espresso as you did, young lady." He then placed a gift on the table and said, "To remember this occasion." Inside the package was an espresso pot with a Lb. of Medalia Doro espresso coffee. We all laughed.

Walking Amelia to the door, he kissed her on the cheek saying, "It was a perfect evening." Then murmured, "Almost perfect."

The knob was carved in white quartz, and the door opened immediately to a wonderland of White Orchid trees. The décor was white and black furniture with touches of chrome, contemporary and fine in its cold elegance. Knowledge whistling while walking toward the window to look out to the sea. When he turned to glance toward me, he had tears in his eyes. Going toward him, taking his arm saying, "Don't be sad."

He reached for my hand speaking, "I wish you didn't cry sad tears ever."

She pushed the button to the large wall screen.

Subtle Seduction

Rain pelting against her window awoke Amelia. She kicked back her covers, got out of bed, and opened her blinds. Sure enough, a dark gray, rainy day on her day off. Outdoor walks and beach stroll ruled out but at home, lots of chores to do. Donning her robe, she thought, "I wonder when I'll meet someone to fall in love with."

This routine of New York travel with mom, living away in an apartment at her worksite is lonely. Remembering that Barry told mom he'd look out for her, but there's only so much a friend can do.

"Oh, my," she said, out loud. A foreboding feeling washed over her. "It's just the dreary day," she pondered. She rose to gather her laundry for the wash and proceed with her domestic goals. It was still raining profusely. She drove to the grocery but still could not shake this dark feeling.

Attempting to cheer up and look forward to dinner with Barry, she decided to shop for a new dress. There is one nice dress shop in town, so Amelia put on a smile and stepped inside. Sandra, the owner, seemed delighted to see her. Trying on several styles, she found one that was elegant in a simple design that was perfect for tonight. She drove home in a better mood than earlier.

Walking into the quiet dark house brought back the foreboding feeling she felt earlier. Attempting to keep busy, she unloaded the groceries. Deciding to clean the kitchen, she then moved to the bathrooms and living room. Up to her elbows in work, the phone rang. It was Barry.

He said, "Just calling to remind you of dinner, and I'll pick you up at 6 o'clock."

Amelia thought, "Gosh, what a big deal over a dinner reservation." Thinking she really wasn't in the mood to go, she thought, "Why didn't I back out? Oh well, something to do."

Remembering how Barry came into her life, she sat down and asked, "How would you like me to show you just how to pay these bills?" There was only one answer at the time as being the wage earner so, in all fairness, I had to find out a method.

He stated, "I can come out on Saturday, and in the meantime, Amelia get together all of the bills."

She did just that, organizing the bills according to companies and dates. At least she was beginning to feel organized with a plan. Little did she know. Again, thinking back, remembering Barry coming by each Saturday, going through the stacks of paper, but it was getting done and Amelia and her mom felt grateful. She liked the aspects of keeping a recorded checking account and the bookkeeping involved. Mom visited a psychiatrist for a short time and before long, had acquired a job. She did so well that she was sent to a trade school and received employment in a home for the blind. It was located on the other shore of the island, so she had to live there through the week since she was the dietician.

Just before she left, Barry asked, "Amelia has done a competent job paying bills and record keeping that I might ask your permission to take her out for a dinner treat."

Although no one asked her, her mother said, "I do believe she deserves it. You may go. Have her home early."

Amelia thought that it is very strange that her mother would give permission to go out with this older man." She didn't feel that she wanted to go but her mother seemed happy about it.

She remembered that Monday at work, Amelia asked Martha, the designer. "What should be worn going to New York for dinner?"

"I'll take you to shop for the little black dress that would be appropriate," said Martha. We found the perfect dress and shoes to feel pretty dressed in. Everyone else seemed happy. She hoped it would be catching. She called her mom, and she could tell her mom was very happy, but Amelia felt very lonely and missed her. The date arrived, and Amelia had a lovely time at the dining experience. After that, when it rained, Barry would pick her up at the train station and take her to fine places for dinner. She was gaining trust with him as a dear friend even though we had a quick peck on the cheek—a kiss goodnight that seemed appropriate.

Her birthday came and went, and Barry was always there with flowers and out to dinner. Then one evening, he said, "The night will be special as I have a wonderful lovely restaurant to take you to on the North Shore of the island by the sea. You will be surprised."

The evening had arrived, and as Amelia slid into the passenger seat, she felt apprehensive again but couldn't imagine why. They had driven for an hour and finally approaching, he said, "Here we have arrived."

Seeing a two-story building curved at the front entrance, surrounded by a brilliant garden and flowing fountain, exclaiming its beauty as Barry held silence. Holding her arm, he ushered her inside to a suite. Opening the door, the room was decorated all in white roses, satin pillows, champagne, and covered food on a table.

"What is all this?" she exclaimed.

He said, "It's our night!"

"But she said . . . I don't want . . . " her words were stopped. Hard kisses covered her mouth forcefully, wet tongue searching, as he skillfully unzipped her dress and unhooked her bra. Devastated, she attempted to fight back, but he was much too strong for her. Throwing her onto the bed, he laid heavily down upon her while his shoulder pinned her down. He skimmed off her panties, and he painfully penetrated her virginity. She cries out as it hurt. There was no love, only possession. He stole what he assumed was his.

He was rolling off of her when he was finished. She could not look at him but went staggering into the bathroom, locking the door. Struggling to get out of the rest of her clothes, she ran the shower to wash off his sweat and smell. After dressing, she sat in a chair while he slept. After a while, he went into the bathroom to shower and dress and came out to sit opposite her.

She asked, "Why did you do this? Do you assume we are getting married?"

He answered, "I have asked my wife for a divorce."

She replied, "I never knew you were married. You have lied to me."

Amelia went to the door, and he followed asking, "Don't you want the flowers?"

"No," was her reply, as tears flowed down her cheeks.

Crying going home, she thought, "Trust for this 'friend' had crashed to rock bottom, and it would take a long time for respect with friendship to rebuild. I've got to get out of here somehow."

Knowledge was anxious to leave this room. "Enough torment," he thought

"Let's leave now!" she voiced.

They left together . . . to approach the next door reaching.

Airborne

The pounding in her brain on how to get away from Long Island. She was seeing things differently since the other night. Dirty and often ugly things. Going into work to New York City awakened her in noticing the wind, stirring up swirling dirt and pieces of paper, cast a final decision for Amelia to leave her modeling jobs and get on a subway to do errands before she left.

Riding the subway rails and looking up at the advertisements, she read about various program incentives for local companies. One caught her interest. There was a bright blue sky with a silver airplane flying among white clouds. Reading across the fuselage it said, "Come Fly With Me!" That did it. A flight attendant. Could it be the answer? She just had to apply and hope. Copying the telephone number, she left for home. When she called, they acknowledged it with an interview appoint. She realized the way to leave home was to become a flight attendant. She felt she could make it with consideration of her height, nice smile, and her personality. We'll see. She hoped they wanted to hire her as much as she wanted the job.

They felt like they needed a reprieve and were delighted to open the opal knobbed door and see an airport terminal."

"To fly away, what a grand idea!" thought Knowledge. He felt better for her and smiled. "Hoping this is a good choice, Amelia!" said Knowledge.

"Me also," Amelia thought.

Back on the train for the city, she crossed her fingers as she hailed a cab to venture forward to the very tall building she encountered. Going up to the thirtieth floor, she walked into the interview room and saw a dozen or more women waiting. She wrote her name next to a number and sat down under a gaze of other hopefuls. Finally called in, the woman who sat opposite her checked her out and then proceeded to ask her questions such as, "How would you feel if a man made a pass at you?" or "Could you prepare a Martini during turbulence?"

Amelia replied, " I guess it would be shaken, not stirred." The interviewer smiled and the interview was over as she was told to wait this week for a call.

She waited, and toward the end of that week, the phone rang. Picking it up on the third ring, she smiled then squealed with delight. She had been accepted and was to fly out to Miami Training School in two weeks. This was just the adventure she needed.

Amelia did not know just how much her world would change. Now to tell her mother. There was nothing at this time to share with Knowledge. He already knew everything. He was delighted this time and brought in champagne and pastries to celebrate. "Fasten your seatbelt," he toasted. We enjoyed our celebration. It was time to consider moving forward toward another door.

There was a family goodbye party and farewell's first. At the airport, when Amelia boarded the flight, she collapsed into the seat of exhaustion. She hoped to be free of her mother and of Barry, two influences that now were unnecessary in her life.

She got a taxi to the school and was welcomed and shown her neat accommodations. Books were handed out with a schedule after a delicious breakfast the next morning. She blended in with the other gals, studying the demonstration of passenger contacts and saving measures. It was an interesting time in which she threw herself completely.

One evening during study, she was paged. She had a visitor. It was Barry. Meeting her in the lobby, they went outside to a bench to talk.

"What do you want" she inquired.

He answered, "I miss you and want you back".

Amelia cried out, "You've got to be kidding! After raping me and lying about a wife you not only lost me but our friendship. I never want to see you again, ever!"

"Please don't leave I'm going through a divorce" he sobbed.

"You've earned it," I replied, and went back inside, shaking with anger. As I got on the elevator, he was still sitting on the bench.

A few weeks after that, Amelia was studying by the pool when a tall, dark, handsome stranger came up and inviting her, he asked: "Would you like to play shuffleboard?"

Looking up, she replied, "Sorry but I don't know how."

He said, "Fine. I'll teach you."

"Alright, for a little break, but I must get back to study," she replied.

He was quiet and some older but very patient. Going back to her seat, he inquired if she could have dinner the next evening, and she said it would be nice.

It was a delightful dinner, and he said goodbye. He had to get back to his home in Atlanta.

Written exams, jumping out of plane exists, lunging onto rafts, practicing all lifesaving procedures came to a final halt for graduation and getting our wings.

A few days before the graduation ceremony, she was told her mother would be flying down. She was the only family member to attend, so when Eagle Airlines found out, they gave her free airfare and a guest room at the inn.

The graduates were given three choices of vases from which to fly out of. All the other gals chose New York, but not Amelia. Not even on my list. My first choice was Dallas as I wanted to be as far away from home as she could get.

My mother, Marie, had a captivating smile and a charm to win you or anyone else over, and she must have used it. She sat next to an executive with the airline coming down to present our wings. That all Amelia needed now as she cringed when they read off the base destinations.

Don't you know I was the ONLY flight attendant to "win" the Atlanta destination. Mother did it once again or could it have been Barry? Reporting in to Crew Schedule was the first step on the second day at home. Flying out was under their control, and the gals to be "nice" to them I was told. Living at home, I was in some way covered from all of that. Mom baked chocolate chip cookies to take reporting in.

This went over big. Mom Marie chatted with them when they called. I received some very great fights and a few furloughs on positive letters of recommendations that came in. I liked the job.

Arriving at LaGuardia Airport one evening, I was met by Barry and another finely attired gentleman, wearing patent shoes and a white silk scarf. He introduced him as his father.

Taking my hand in, looked into my eyes, he asked, "Do you love my son?"

Glancing directly back into his, saying, "No, he lost my assumed friendship and took extreme advantage of me. All respect for him is gone."

He drew my hand and kissed it, saying, "He will not bother you anymore."

"Thank you," I replied and walked away.

This was a surprise encounter causing her hand to tremble as she reached for her keys. She waited for a while just to make sure she wasn't being followed.

It was discovered in her files she supposed that she had been a model. Eagle Airlines began using her for promotions. Handing out orange juice at the Catskill resorts, flying in circles to hand out champagne for first-class meals served in minutes to introduced new aircraft. This caused her paycheck to diminish as the flight time had been cut and they refused extra promotion fees. She lost money and gratification and decided she would be leaving soon.

In the meantime, Amelia had a few flights to Atlanta and visited Joel. One day, she had to spend overnight in Atlanta with the crew, so she called him. They agreed to have a picnic and hike to Stone Mountain. Early that morning, she dashed out for some shorts and hiking shoes with a sigh of relief. It was a beautiful warm day and on up the steep climb they advanced.

"This is a perfect stop to make for lunch," he reported.

"Perfect as there must be water in that case," she replied.

Joel brushed off a rock for her while she noticed the perfect view of Atlanta. So beautiful. They were both hungry, so they ate in a quiet place.

When finished, Joel asked, "Do you like Atlanta?"

"Oh, yes. It would have been nice to have been based here away from home. I must leave the airlines now as the pay has dropped but SAS has shown some interest."

Joel got silent and reached inside his pocket, pulling out a small black box. Taking her hand, he asked, "Would you like to be my wife and live in Atlanta?"

Wow! She was so surprised and silent, searching for an answer she thought, "Didn't she want to leave New York? Did she not like this man? I guess he thought about provision as she'd have to quit her job. She enjoyed their few dates. He wasn't fresh or forward perhaps because he was older, settled."

Finally she answered, "OK."

Joel flew up to New York and met Amelia's mother on their eleventh date. The introductions were made, and as Joel sat down, her little dog "Luckie" jumped up on his lap and peed all over his clothes. Joel yelled, "If you think you're bringing this dog to my house, you're mistaken!" He was very angry.

Later, Mom said to me, "Is this an omen, Honey?" Once again, she so much missed her daddy and his advice.

On one of her last flights, she was an attendant in an old DC-3 flying its last flight to Canada. There were only three crew members: a captain, co-pilot, and Amelia. It would be a fast layover with no time or place for tours only sleep, to leave in the morning. We disembarked, and the co-pilot took our luggage, placing it on the cart. We rode to the cabins that looked quaint. Thinking he was being a gentleman, he then reached for my bag as she opened the door.

Going inside with it, he pushed me in, closing the door with his foot. My glace at him froze as I noticed the look on his face with its evil grin. He grabbed her arm and threw her onto the bed when she braced her knee up at his groin for protection. He then slapped her hard across the face, calling out, "Bitch, you know you want me!"

She was ready to fight. He must have sensed she could and went out the door slamming it hard enough for the walls to shake. Trembling and terrified, she locked the doors and checked the windows before she fell down on the bed. She fell asleep and woke up the next morning hungry.

Still afraid, she met the captain having breakfast. He looked at her with a curious stare, asking, "What happened? Why the red mark on your face?"

The co-pilot wasn't there, so she told him the whole story.

"I'm glad you had the courage to tell me. Don't worry. I'll report this as soon as we land in New York. You'll be informed by my report."

Two weeks later, Amelia received a letter from Eagle Airlines confirming that this was not the first complaint turned in about this co-pilot and he had been fired. A personal note added not to worry about any retaliation from him as he had no information on her nor would any be released.

Several days later, Crew Schedule called with happy news. There is a furlough trip to Virgin Islands with airfare and accommodations included. They sure took care of their own.

"Destiny deals with our choices and fate attempts to set us straight," said Knowledge, "Time to ... "

11 Honeymoon

Amelia had second thoughts. Perhaps she was running away. It's just my nerves as she looked at the calendar. Only a few dates and then marriage?

"Do I really know him? What's to know?" I thought.

"This day is our wedding day and twelfth time to be together." She mumbled. She started to shake as she threw cold water on her face. Her cousin came in, noticing her raw nerves and turned on some music to calm her. Checking her suitcase, Madge, her cousin, noticed that she had everything but a contraceptive.

"Oh my gosh!" Madge spoke. "We have to dash out to the drugstore immediately! Let's go!" Amelia hurried behind Madge and pulled up in front of the store. The owner was there and walked back with them, recommending a Douche Bag. He pulled out a pink one which was quickly purchased and later crammed into her suitcase.

A lovely clear autumn day, the wedding went along smoothly as it was planned. There was dancing, cake cutting, champagne and then time to leave. Suddenly Amelia got a knot in her stomach, and didn't want to go. She was frightened. Who was this stranger? Marie noticed her daughter's hesitation and went to her to hug.

"It will be alright. I'll come to visit over the holidays and you can come home anytime."

Amelia fought back tears. The hugs and goodbyes made the pit of her stomach hurt.

"Oh, Daddy!" she sniffled.

It was a long wordless drive into the city. He parked at this small hotel, and Amelia and Jack were ushered into a small room containing twin beds. She was fatigued and relieved when she saw them, thinking, "He'll sleep and not bother me tonight. Good." She then went into the bathroom to change into her nightgown.

It was dark when she came out. Jack was in bed sound asleep, she thought. Quietly taking the other bed, Amelia slid down into the covers when they were suddenly tossed back, her nightgown thrown up, and bam he threw himself heavily on top and roughly went into her. No caresses, no love expressions just wham, bam! It hurt her body and her heart as she lay in the sticky, wet mess.

Going into her suitcase to retrieve the douche bag, she went into the bathroom and closed the door. He hadn't even spoken to her. Oh, she's hurt!

Unwrapping the pink bag, she read the directions. It said, "Fill the bag up with lukewarm water and hang it at a high level. As she took it to move away from the sink, the hose cut loose and whipped all over the bathroom. There was water everywhere. As she tried to grab it, she slipped, fell, and hit her head on the toilet, but did not pass out. Feeling dizzy, the tears poured down her cheeks. Sitting in the mess for a while, she thought of her dad.

"I miss you," she said, through her tears. "I'm sorry too, God. My naïve decisions have turned, but I've given a promise, and I will try to be a good wife. There's always tomorrow."

Attempting to calm down, she cleaned up, then as silent as possible, slipped into the rumpled bed with distaste. Amelia awoke as Jack had dressed and was leaving to go downstairs for breakfast. He said, "I'll wait for you downstairs." Those were the first worst words since yesterday.

Amelia felt some better after a good breakfast. They got into Jack's car and proceeded to Maryland. She was surprised to arrive at a boat dock where Jack had placed a small motorboat with water skis for their honeymoon trip.

Jack stated, "This is our new boat as we will travel in it down the Inland Waterway to South Carolina."

It sounded like fun. So off we went, leaving the car for his friend to pick up and drive to the town where we'll end up. They cruised and skied days stopping at small motels by the water at night.

"He was always exhausted," Amelia thought, so I didn't get touched and no romance but the days were fun. There was one crazy time when the tide went out stranding us. We had to use our skis to move us out, but it took a very long exhausting time. Another time was during a storm in Charleston Harbor. We were trying to get in, but the waves pulled us back and that was also a long fretful experience. We made it exhaustedly. We were at our destination. The car was there, and our aching body got in to drive to Atlanta.

As Amelia headed to a home, she didn't know her stomach did flip-flop whatever lay ahead.

Jack's home was two stories, with a deck from the kitchen over the garage. They were greeted by neighbors. A party was given by new friends across the street. The "poking" resumed as Jack literally rolled over on top at night, and when finished, rolled back. No words, no warnings, just a f—k.

It didn't happen very often. He traveled starting Monday until Friday, so reality settled in for Amelia. She wanted a home, so she bought a decorating and cook book home and began to make this house a home. She enjoyed cooking so she fed Jack well and entertained friends. Looking for a church was a quest, but Jack said he would not go with her. She started adding some softness to the house and Jack was very pleased. They at least were friends.

One night after dinner, Jack suggested taking a trip out west. He'd need a new car and started looking. I suggested he look at Volkswagens as that is what served me so well, especially for long drives. It's engine was air-cooled and very good on gasoline.

He later came home to tell Amelia about a Renault he saw and liked. I said I'd love to see it, so he drove it home three days later saying he bought it and its color was pea green. Ugh, but his money, his choice. My input was useless.

It was a great time. Inspiring such as the Maroon Bell Mountains in Colorado, Grand Canyon, Brice Canyon, and Yellowstone Park. While driving across the Arizona Desert going back, the Renault cracked an engine in the extreme heat. Amelia didn't say a word but knew the air-cooled engine wouldn't have done that. They had to abandon the car and take a long bus ride home. All the way, Amelia had nausea and thought it was from the bumpy motion and heat. But . . . Amelia was pageant.

Happy she was for now, she'd have someone to love.

Time to address a project: the baby's room. We had a spare bedroom that would be perfect, so one day, opening the closet to clean it out, a few small boxes fell on the floor, spilling its contents. Picking them up, I noticed photographs of a nude woman on a blanket on the floor. Getting frightened realizing how little we knew of each other, she felt sick. She tried to remain calm, and that weekend it was time to talk. He came home that Friday to a lost, blank look on Amelia's face that said, "Now what? I need an explanation."

He explained, "I had been married before to an alcoholic so divorce was inevitable. I forgot I had those pictures. I'm sorry."

He just didn't act sorry. Our life went on and Amelia's tummy grew with her precious one. It's all she felt she had, and hoped it would be enough.

There was a baby shower given by neighbors and friends. Punch, tiny sandwiches, and a lovely cake were served. There were also games and giggles as well as multiple gifts galore.

Decorating the room was a joy. Attempting to complete the canopy curtains one night, she felt energetic and volunteered to go bowling with the crew that bowled. Taking a shower, she suddenly noticed warm water down her thighs which meant her water broke. It was three weeks ahead of schedule, but she stepped out and dried off when the first contraction arrived.

"No bowling tonight!" Jack stated, as he helped Amelia into the car.

He said, "I hope all is alright because I need to stop for gas."

"Certainly, who knew the baby was ready early?" Amelia replied.

They were at the hospital none too soon.

"She is here! A perfect beautiful girl," the doctor called out.

Amelia now felt a touch of heaven!

Amelia smiled at Knowledge, saying, "She was worth all of it. I'm in love with this wee one."

Adventure

The sounding horn from the sleek cruise, Vulcania, called passengers to come aboard. It was time. Amelia, in her bright new travel clothes, walked excitedly up the canopied gang plank only to see her aunt and uncle who arrived to see her off. What a surprise! They were guided to her cabin where there was champagne provided and cheers for good wishes to celebrate. There was stoic admiration that Amelia felt, that she was embarking with some family on this adventure.

The whistle soon sounded again for visitors to leave. Walking out on deck to wave farewell, they leaned over the rail to wave as the gangplank was removed. Streamers were thrown and balloons were hoisted. It was all colorful and grand. The band played as the ship was being tugged out into the harbor. The Statue of Liberty stood regally, overlooking the entrance to the harbor as the skyline faded as we continued to sail to the Atlantic Ocean. Luncheon chimes rang to call us in to enjoy fine food for lunch. This enjoyment continued the entire trip.

The ship's captain sat most often at our family table, telling us tales of the sea. Amelia soon felt a pang of homesickness for her daughter. It was nice to conclude the day by walking along the outside deck to look at the sky full of stars. Amelia would say a prayer, put it to a star and send it home to her girl.

Amelia had grown familiar with the sea, through sailing, swimming, and noticing the ocean's ebbs and flows. A strong north wind storm hit a few days out that wasn't frightening to her, nor did she experience the seasickness that hit almost everyone else on board. Her aunt and uncle were experiencing this and were taking medication for it, staying in their cabin.

One night, there were ropes along the wall put up so people could walk, she guessed. She used these ropes to guide her into the dining room. Walking into the room, Amelia saw that it was empty except for three waiters surprised, standing along the serving table. One waiter escorted her to a table supplied with pulled up edge that was purposefully placed to keep the plates from sliding off.

She proceeded to order coffee to sip on until they served the meatball spaghetti dish with salad.

The ship continued to roll as the other two waiters left. The waiter who took my order came out with a large tray and, as if in slow motion, the ship listed in a roll to one side as the waiter dipped down, Amelia in her chair lifted out of the seat being caught by the waiters left shoulder while he held the tray with his right.

"What a ballet!" she acclaimed. As the ship righted, she thanked the waiter and proceeded to retire to her room when the waiter came out to hand her a bag containing rolls and cheese. They both smiled, and she thanked him with a big smile.

The storm eventually subsided and everything came back to its normal place. Noticing aunt Lou as she stored roll, cheese and meat in her almost huge carpet-type bag was in wonder about it. Arriving in Lisbon, out first port, we had four hours to disembark if desired. Aunt Lou and buggy ride onto cobblestone streets to town and all the shops and restaurants were closed from two p.m. until four p.m. every day for siesta. Now to find out about Aunt Lou's bag. Borrowing the carriage blanket, she picked out a Hillside to spread out lunch. She even brought a bottle of wine. It was perfect and taught me a lot about travel in style.

One evening in the shops, the captain stopped by their table to announce a Greek party taking place and invited us all to go. The other back off but aunt Lou said she'd like to go if Amelia would. Saying yes, she got up from the table to follow the captain. There were no other blonds there, so Amelia stood out, noticing a tall, slim young man staring at her. Approaching her, he took her elbow as he escorted her and her aunt to a seat, bowed and smiled. Then the men formed a circle and began the most graceful and energetic dance she had ever seen. The young man came over to her and her aunt, offering a glass of ouzo. It was delicate and delicious and enjoyed the second when aunt said it was time to leave. We were escorted back toward our room by the young man and was given a kiss on the hand. It was a lovely experience.

Amelia will never forget his coal-black eyes set against the snow-white skin, the waves of his black hair, nor the warmth of his lips when he kissed her hand. There was a fire in his look when he said goodnight. Fine time!

The next day, the cruise ship passed the Rock of Gibraltar which looked powerful surrounded by strong waves crashing on the shore—the entrance to the Mediterranean countries. We had made the voyage with delight as this was a chilling experience. There were only two hours if one wanted to disembark, and we wanted to mix and mingle in the quaintness of it all. The day was dark, and every place seemed wet with sea spray. We enjoyed the feeling and stopped by a bench to enjoy another picnic.

The next day was sunny as we crossed into the crescent-shaped harbor in Naples, Italy where Mt. Vesuvius stood proudly in the background. One didn't find it hard to imagine the eruption that covered Pompeii so many years ago. The city was covered in ash for centuries since 79 A.D.

The guide proudly stated, "The excavation started in 1861 and did notice that the deepest tracks uncovered went to the House of Prostitution. The walls there were still brilliant with colors of red, black and yellow, with carvings of carriages and other relics of history. This city was then shaped in an oval design of two miles in diameter. The vivid art of the walls defied imagination. Magnificent!"

The color of the waters of the Mediterranean Sea on the way to Patras, Greece was aquamarine. This tour stirred Amelia's imagination for the toga-dressed Greeks long ago in 776 B.C. riding in their chariots. The columns of the temples and the coliseums were enormous! The site was destroyed in 476 A.D. and covered by a river for 1,300 years. Mind-boggling!

Returning to the ship, Amelia and her aunt saw the lovely city bathed in colored lights, reflecting on the water. It was a nostalgic farewell. Above her out on board, she noticed her Greek gentleman wave goodbye as they were disembarking. She acknowledged his wave then he blew a kiss her way as he stepped upon the gangplank.

She mouthed, "Adieu," and thought, "Lovely Greece."

The arrival to Venice, Italy was at dawn. Aunt Lou and Amelia were up to gaze at the sunrise entrance and watch the luminous shades of lavender, pink, and gold change position, making way for the sunrise. The colors awakened the city's waterways, winding around old, graceful building and homes, looking as if they sat in the water. Beautiful gondolas made their way to us, bringing us to our hotel from the ship as we said our adieus to all we met.

Our gondola guided by oars were in rhythm of songs sung by our oarsman. How romantic it was, the beautiful old city of music and grace. We spent two time-filled days in Venice seeing the magnificent Church of San Marco, the pigeon-laden square and stopped in many party shops for hot chocolate in the mornings and afternoon Italian Espresso with one lump of sugar and a strip of lemon peel. Perfect! Complete in happiness, the best was yet to come.

If you could imagine her, Amelia would be this pretty blonde-haired woman with shining blue eyes and tall slim body dressed differently and always noticeable. February is the peak of fashion scene in Europe. The rich and the poor were dressed alike—black! Amelia had chosen bright yellow for her coat and suitcase. Imagine how she unexpectedly stood out. She was looked at, whistled to, and pinched. Who knew! She simply watched and listened to all she was learning. She noticed the charm and polite attitude of Italian women.

Completely happy with all this, she didn't realize that the best was still to come. They had to travel with luggage in hand to catch the inner trains through the country. It was all intriguing! They had found quaint hotel by the Arno River in which to stay. Nearby was the Ponte Vecchio bridge they could see from their balcony while enjoying breakfast. Aunt Lou held a city map for us to check for our stroll through. Aunt Lou had seen it all so she begged me out and sent me to explore on my own. I discovered the Baptistery brass doors by artist Giovanni and the fine art in the Uffizi Gallery which took one whole day. Aunt Lou was pleased with my discoveries. Then she entered the academia where Michelangelo's sculpture "David" was supposed to be. It was a small gallery with one long narrow hall. Going down the hall, turning a corner, it was right there in a room with glass ceiling for natural light. Amazing! She was struck with awe! Never has she seen such perfect beauty. This sight was the whole trip for her. David was a brain explosion for her. Such beauty! The tears simply flowed down her face as she stood frozen in time. Not realizing how long she stood still, she knew she had to move. She did slowly, not willing to disturb her emotion. She knew that now. She walked to a different drumbeat!

Aunt Lou, the persistent traveler, said, "We cannot miss the lovely town to Sienna, Italy as it was just a Taxi drive up to a small town." So off they ventured. A beautiful glass-stained windowed cathedral stood in the town center surrounded by individual shops. Since the train ride to Rome would be four hours, they chose to pull out the carpet bag and equip it for lunch train ride picnic. The fabulous meal of cheeses, breads, pastry, and wine was now standard delicious fare that couldn't be beat. Yum!

Before they left the town, they were treated to view a jousting on a house back game exhibition which was an eyeful of excitement. Time now to leave for the train.

Aunt Lou reminded us saying, "Don't bring what you can't run with, including suitcases." We found out why. The train to catch was several tracks over, and we had to run as it was waiting for us. Run we did!

Panting, we were glad we listened. Sitting back for our ride, we enjoyed lunch. The city of Rome was a spectacle of grandiosity. Thrilled by the coliseum that once held gladiators from 82 A.D., the Patheon Temple, Trevi Fountain where we tossed coins, Piazza di Spagna, a favorite spot of Keats and Shelley. There is history that goes on and on in this city.

They did not forget to visit the Vatican City museums and Sistine Chapel Ceiling by Michaelangelo and also his Statue of Moses. There is incredible art in the stained-glass windows of cathedrals. With the constant activity of catching buses and trains, carrying our own luggage, and miles of sightseeing, any excess weight gained on board the ship was lost. Memories were multiplied.

Flying over the snow-covered Alps from Rome to Paris was a natural sight of beauty below. Arriving at a quaint French hotel in Paris, we had two last days to explore. We all went to the French flea market where Louise had made contact to work and buy for her antique shop in New Hope, Pennsylvania. This market covered a long block in size. The contents were beautiful vintage collections from Europe. It was an interesting process watching aunt Lou work. She would slap a piece of I.D. on the item she wished sent to her.

We had enough energy left to catch a taxi up to Montmartre to observe artists at work and to gaze at a beautiful view of the city of Paris. They continued to stroll, covering the Champs-Elysees, saw the Museum of Modern Art, and the Notre Dame Cathedral. Another day they visited the Louvre which took the day. Leaving, they walked the Grand Boulevards, ate at Rumble Meyers, walked through the Tuileries Gardens and then fell into bed for some needed rest. They were exhausted but happy. Ready for home!

Amelia heart was heavy thinking about all she had experienced as she boarded the Air France jet. Something had changed in her, and her new friend aunt Lou, knew it!

Knowledge said, "Wow! Nice experience. Your aunt Lou had insights into you that I guess you never knew. What an experience! Your wisdom instincts have begun to kick in. I know there are changes that will happen to you."

Amelia smiled and said, "Time to travel forward. Let's go!"

Before entering the net door, Knowledge said, "Let's go to the dining room for I've prepared a dinner for you to enjoy, as you'll soon be going on a journey and will need energy. Amelia was ready for this invitation for she enjoyed his cooking. Having completed a delightful feast, they were content when they approached the brown topaz doorknob. Waiting, her car was with full gas tank and she cleaned up as was usual.

The Yellow Rose

The lines of the highway were like strips of adhesive pressed between Amelia's eyes as she watched the road's direction north. On a mission stopping at a motel for a fit-full few hours, never having driven for seventeen hours.

She was on a quest to find out what was happening as the last time she spoke with Megan, her stomach went into knots. Megan's voice was weak and she murmured in a frightened tone. She needed help... now!

Throwing some personal items and snacks into the car, Amelia roared off. She stayed within speed limits but pushed when safe to do so through the light rain for she couldn't afford the time for being stopped. Knowing where Megan lived, she pulled up in front and pried her fingers from the steering wheel. Knocking on the door that morning, she heard a commanding man's voice ordering Megan to see who it was. She cracked open the door with a space just wide enough for a peek. At first glance, her dirty robe was noticeable as her hollow dark eyes. When she saw her mom, she flew open the door and collapsed into her arms saying, "Oh, Momma," and cried.

Then suddenly catching herself, she stood upright to say, "What are you doing here?"

She ducked back inside as Amelia called out, "Wait! I drove up here to take you both out to breakfast."

Megan stiffened straight, owning that she was dealing with something evil and had to be cautious. "Coming up this way to visit old friends and stopping by to see you."

She lied, a deep voice from inside said, "Who is that?"

Megan closed the door as she spoke to him, explaining the situation. A few minutes later, she reappeared saying, "That's fine. We'll meet you there as we have to dress."

"I'll wait," I replied.

Amelia slid down the wall near the door as she noticed a fire escape along the end hall where he could flee. The purpose was to see him face to face. This was a strength she had from within. Sometime later, they came out into the hall. Megan made introductions, but he wouldn't look at Amelia. Knowledge of him grew as we sat down in a booth. He sat opposite as Amelia attempted to keep a sweet motherly tone even while wanting to punch him out. Expressing this sweet tone, she voiced how they missed Megan. Stressing how everyone wanted to see her and meet him. Amelia had a plan she told them. The waitress took our order and left when Amelia looked at her daughter and noticed a yellowish bruise on her face under her eye. Quelling the sudden anger that rose in her veins, she noticed him kick her under the table when asking, "What happened?"

Megan looked down at her hands while he made up a story. Answering, he said, "Oh, a big spider bit her, but it's healing."

Knowing he was lying, Amelia stared at him with the look, piercing into his brain that he flew back against the seat that almost went over and yelled, "Get her off me!"

Engulfed in fear, he jumped up saying "I have to go to work."

Flying out the door with speed, we both knew what was up. Megan was hungry and finished eating. Sipping on coffee, Amelia spoke again about her coming home. My precious daughter looked like hell, but she was my angel.

"I can't. He said he would kill you and my family in Georgia if I left."

I said, "We can do this. We can get help."

Excusing myself and calling the pastor who was contacted earlier, explaining further that my daughter was kidnapped and held hostage and experiencing fear that freezes action. He said he would look into this and return my call.

Megan said she had to get back and should leave. They walked in, though as Amelia was thinking that hell would freeze over before she left her daughter. Going with her into the apartment, Amelia was shocked at the filth and destruction as only evil can do. Not saying much, Amelia offered to help clean up and Megan hugged her. The hug reminded her of her weakness from torment. There was an impulse to put down and that was to grab her and run. The call came in from the pastor just in time, for he told me to be careful of just that instinct. It had to be Megan's own will or there could be kidnap charge. In the process of assisting her, I gathered up dirty clothes and towels and carried them into the basement to wash in the machines. Taking them back upstairs, I met at the door with Megan standing there trembling.

She said, "Mom, you have to leave right now."

"Why?"

"He's on the way now with a dead rat! This means death!" she cried out.

I replied, "I will go back to the hotel and stay and wait to hear from her if she would. In the meantime, just get a few personal things ready." Telling her there was a friend here who knew how to protect us, and I wasn't afraid.

But she said "no" again as my heart sank. Amelia simply said, "I would wait for her at the hotel until she changed her mind."

Packing and praying while sitting waiting for the phone, it finally rang. It was Megan, frantic. "I'm going with you! Hurry over. He went to get a gun!" Grabbing my suitcase, I threw money to pay my bill on the counter and zoomed over the apartment. Megan was standing outside and jumped into the car, yelling, "Go!" Amelia called for help immediately as they left.

When they arrived to get on the highway, there were patrol cars waiting to catch him, protecting us. One police car followed us a way on the escape that we felt safe at last. The flood of relief came over Megan as she sat and cried. Later stopping for gas, Megan got out of the car and fainted, crumbling in my arms. She whispered, "Oh Mom, I think I'm pregnant." Getting her something to eat and drink made her feel better as we resumed driving home.

"When did you decide to go with me? It had to be your decision."

It was after you called this morning to speak to us. He threw a cup of hot coffee on me and stormed out. He said, 'I'll finish this.' I knew he went for a gun, and I knew right then to get out."

"Honey, you are now free, and together with God, we can do this."

PHASE TWO:

The more miles of space from New York, the more courage pumps through Megan's veins. She felt strong enough now to assist driving, helping her Mom take a break. They were both relieved and happy driving south toward Atlanta, with the family waiting for them. It was midnight driving up to Amelia's apartment. Collapsing inside, she decided to go right to bed and shower in the morning. We did! Goodness, grace, and mercy prevailed.

The next day, Amelia explained to Megan about the house she was having built. She told her about the extra bedroom and bath for her and the baby. Relieved hugs were multiplied, and the hugs went on for a while. The refrigerator was empty so they went out to breakfast and stopped by to see the new home. Megan was enthralled, and on the way back, stopped for groceries. All was well. Playing lovely soothing music to keep emotions calm, it would be truly good when Megan would no longer cry out, "No. No. Stop!"

We kept busy planning the décor and furniture for our home. Megan was excited with the white crib for the baby and enjoyed fixing her room. One day, Megan grabbed my arm. Grimacing, she said, "The baby's coming. Let's go!"

We dashed off cautiously to the hospital as fast as we could go. Megan wanted natural childbirth, so she had to keep walking. When the labor pain arrived, she'd grip my arm until it hurt and said, "Ouch!" Her timing was short now, so up on the delivery table they placed her.

Letting me keep my arms around her shoulders, it wasn't very long before the doctor called out, "Here she is! A beautiful baby girl!" He handed her to Amelia while he finished with Megan. As soon as she was able, I gave her over, and we both had streaming tears of joy! At peace with her daughter safe, Amelia got busy planning for the move. Megan helped, and together, it was a happy atmosphere.

Knowledge opened the door for her this time.

"There are things that happen that could be called miracles. Here are two events so called because of their nature," Knowledge said.

"Who knew!" spoke Amelia. "There are at least three truthfully to include, such as "The Yellow Rose," She arose from her chair to go out to the double doors and notice the diamond doorknobs.

Rescued from Drowning

Near Atlanta was a lovely lake hotel. Amelia and her husband thought it would be a nice idea to go to dinner there and stay over as they had an early morning appointment for lake sailing lessons. Amelia had only sailed in open waters so lake sail would be approached differently. Saul seemed happy about the idea. In the early morning, sunshine was coming through the window and woke Amelia. She remembered the pool near the lobby and thought a quick swim would be delightful. She arrived downstairs but found the doors locked to the outside pool. Noticing an opening between the two pools, she got into the inside one and moved forward to jump through the opening.

"Ready, set, and go!" she spoke only. *Bam!* She dove too deeply and struck her head on something, knocking her senseless. Suddenly, a pair of arms reached down for her, bringing her to the surface and leaned her across the edge. Her eyes refocused, and she could see a figure in a brown suit going down to the end of the hall and turn the corner. She called out but was still fuzzy-headed, she got back into the water thinking, "I've got to try again!" She did, but this time diving deeper, she scraped her face on the bottom. Getting to the surface, she saw blood on her hand and said, "That does it." She got out, wrapping herself in a towel.

She went upstairs to meet Saul for breakfast. Not saying about her experience, she enjoyed a wonderful breakfast. Then it was time to go out and "Learn How to Sail" as the brochure read. It was a great day, and we did learn some things about sailing. Thinking then, she'd wait until another long island venture. It was a good trip.

"It was a bright, beautiful day the last time you defied fate," said Knowledge. "You preserve like a diamond and leave many dazzled."

Light streamed through the slates of the Venetian blinds, another day was breaking. Slowly, Amelia stretched long in her bed, then opened her eyes to greet the morning. Something was weird. Her left eye was stuck shut and her right eye opened a slit, obviously in sympathy with its partner. Drat! Pink eye! She exclaimed getting out of bed. She took a clean cloth and ran hot water. Attempting to soak the eye, she bathed it and made a compress. She waited for the sticky mess to clear. Under the layer of gunk, she knew an inevitable "pink pimple" would be appearing on her eyelid, taking days to disappear.

After fifteen minutes of attempts to open her eye, response was minimal. This definitely was not a normal case of pink eye. Time to call the doctor. Told to come right in, she did. The doctor looked hum'med and haw'ed and put some eye drops in her eye.

"That should do it. Here are some steroid drop for every four hours to kill the infection," he professed, and sent her home. That night, she awoke in eye pain that was horrific! It would not quit, so the first thing she did was call the doctor.

"Come right in!" they said. She opened the office door and was immediately ushered into an exam room. There was a visiting eye doctor in and her original doctor invited him to examine her eye. "Well," he stated, "looks like you may have scratched your cornea, and I need to have a specialist look at it. Are you free today?"

"Yes," I replied, anxious to have a good opinion. Hastily, Amelia called her office to postpone appointments for the day.

When she returned to the exam room, the doctor had his back toward her, scheduling her in soon as possible. She heard. "I contacted a specialist, Dr. Arnold, and he will see you immediately."

A sense of dread filled her head and heart as she made her way across town to meet a diagnosis she certainly didn't want to hear.

"What is wrong?" she announced, sitting down in the chair.

"Let's see," he replied. Looking at her eye long and hard, he wheeled back and stated, "It seems you have a serious optic infection that is attacking the optic nerve and will progress to the right eye as well. This infection or virus moves very rapidly, and there is currently no cure. You will eventually go blind."

Amelia sat stunned. She shuddered attempting to get words out, "How long do I have?"

"The loss of sight will be gradual, although you will notice your peripheral vision going first. This vision will cloud over, taking a day or two or month or so."

"Tomorrow there is a plan for me to go to the Conyers Monastery and spend a weekend in prayer. Driving myself is what is done to get there. Is that alright?"

"Shouldn't be a problem, but if you go and notice you peripheral sight disappearing, call your family right away and have someone bring you in to my office immediately."

A thick gauze patch was placed over my eye to help her good eye focus while driving. She knew navigating the roads may be more difficult but prayed others too would be careful. As she approached the monastery gate, she noticed that the left eye vision was foggy.

"Oh, no." She gulped. It's happening fast. What will the children think as they should not be scared like she was right now. A strange feeling of flight filled her whole body as she checked in. Given a room, she was told that in five minutes, vesper services would begin. She removed the eye patch before going into the chapel, wishing to experience the host of shadows, knowing soon her eyesight would be covered in blackness. If ever she needed solace, it was now! As was the custom, those with her were called forward to go up front as there was a visiting priest to greet. She slid up, grasping for a free hand to hold, but it wasn't enough. Amelia tripped on a forward step bumping into the priest knocking the chalice of holy water he held gently. The water went all over, including into her face, eye, and everywhere. Amelia was mortified but then moving over to the side door started to laugh.

"Oh, God! You have a sense of humor. What else could hit me in the eye. I'm not complaining. At least I have all the rest of my senses: taste, sight, and touch. Thank you, Father, for all of my blessings."

She prayed and went to sleep. The next morning as Amelia eased into wakefulness, she listened to birdsongs and smelled the sweet fragrance of lilacs seeping through her open window. Stirring suddenly, realizing bright sunshine was coming in her window, she bounced out of bed calling out "Hallelujah!" She could see just fine indeed. She looked in the mirror, saw the furnishings around her and got down on her knees to give thanks! She called the doctor with the news, and he wanted her to come in as soon as possible. She knew she had been truly blessed and kept praying up, giving thanks all the way to the office.

Amelia was ushered in to have her eyes checked. It was a long checkup and Dr. Arnold did not speak a word. "Don't worry, this check takes a while. I want to be certain." Dr. Arnold finally announced that the eyes were clear and cured, and her vision test at 20/20.

The doctor then slammed his down on the counter and said, "That does it! My wife has invited me to church with her for years. Now I'm going."

Later that day, Amelia called the priest to apologize and told him the story. He then requested that she write the story to be placed inside the "Book of Miracles" that is beside bed stands in the room. She did and it was there the last time she visited.

"It takes faith to suppose in miracles, and it's personal," said Knowledge. "Trials turn into wisdom which makes me a great friend!"

One day, the heart is ready to express love and a prince appears. The couples are whisked away in a dream world and reality. Then, greed from man's nature displays itself, and it is all gradually lost. Knowledge reveals this as he and Amelia enter the opal doorknob.

The Fall of Camelot

Surprised at the confidence in the woman's voice he asked forthright questions. His niece had been a model and suggested he call Amelia. Saul had seen her in the fashion newspapers and thinking she was right, called. He was being refused.

"Oh, dear," she commented on his request for dinner.

Amelia explained, "There is a pageant during the weekend, and she is running it so must work on it."

He then replied, "He'd call again,"

About to walk into the kitchen, the phone rang again. It was her friend from Tennessee, Miss Knoxville.

"Hi, Amelia. I'm stuck in a motel and need to get out. Can you meet me for dinner?"

"No," I said. "There is someone looking for a date that I couldn't make tonight. Are you interested?"

"I haven't met him, do you?"

"Oh, sure," she said. "I've got to get out!"

Over the phone, those two met and made arrangements for the evening.

The pageant went well and "Miss Stone Mountain" was selected. Then my phone rang next morning. One call was to thank me for the date with such a beautiful woman and the other from my girlfriend saying, "Thanks for the date with a gentleman."

When he called me back, he said he really wanted to take me out to dinner. The only other available time was at the finale of fashionatta. That evening, we all wanted to go out to celebrate, and he could meet up with us. Everyone was pleased. He made a hit with all, adding his charm across the tables. Our dating began. The fall season was upon us and his brother shared 50yd. seats at the Ga. Tech football games. What fun! What was especially enjoying was Friday night meals at the Mother and Father's home. The table sat eighteen of us, and there were two cooks in the kitchen and a man who served. We were busy with family and friends and they all loved my two pretty daughters. It didn't seem like many months had passed, but we were falling in love. Saul asked me to marry him with everyone's wishes, so I received an engagement ring to sparkle on my finger. Happiness prevailed as Amelia now had a big family. The prince and princess would now reign over their kingdom and hoped to live happily ever after.

Saul and his brother were in the clothing design business, and Amelia did fashion shows for community efforts. One afternoon, the director of Israel's Fashion called Amelia. There was to be an international show, and they were interested in Amelia directing it. She did put it all together smoothly, immediately. She made all the decisions and plans on the fashion, models, runway, lighting and music. She wrote scripts for everyone to use during rehearsal. There were no mishaps, and it was a thrilling success. Amelia was then approached by the Israel team that flew in to see the show. Invited to run the big international European show in Israel as the host country, Amelia was certainly surprised and thrilled. They would hire interrupters but wanted Amelia to handle stage design, scripts, lighting—all the details of the show.

That evening, conveying all this good news to Saul, he said, "No! definitely not! I need you here."

"Why?" she asked.

"Because of the children," he replied.

I answered, "But they will go with me and go to school for only two months. It will be such a grand experience for all of us."

I couldn't understand his anger nor his profound refusal. I feel let down all week and sad as even his brother couldn't change his mind. Feeling tired of arguing, it wasn't the answer as we got nowhere. It was finally dropped, and Amelia refused to do any more gratis shows. A few months after, Saul suggested we do some traveling. We went to visit England, Sweden, Spain, Norway, Switzerland, and Holland. The brilliant lights and sights, restaurants were fine. It was happy and romantic.

Amelia missed two menstrual cycles when she got home, so went to the doctor who announced her as pregnant. With this confirmation, she planned a special evening. Champagne, steaks, and a favorite desert, she also felt very pretty. After their meal, she picked up her glass for a toast.

"Here's to you as you're to be a new daddy!"

"What? No! You'll have to have an abortion." I almost dropped my glass and took a hold of the chair as the room swayed. "I don't want any more children!" he yelled out.

"Tell me something understandable!" cried Amelia.

He shouted out, "We're too old to have a baby! Never!" And stormed out of the house.

She sat down dazed, remembering over the past four years of trying. Coming back drunk, she questioned the respect she had always had for him.

"Oh, my God!" She thrust her head into the pillow and cried herself to sleep. Looking back, it was the night he left her. There were all the signs. He rarely talked or took her out, ignored her at family dinners. Sometimes we went to the club, but he wouldn't dance nor talk to me. It was strange feeling disowned. She did love Saul so very much but this dug into her soul, refusing the abortion no matter what. When our baby girl was born, he seemed to take some interest, and Amelia's hopes grew. Our little girl had a soaring smile that captivated everyone's heart. Since the family welcomed her, Amelia thought they'd be back on track.

Saul took interest in tennis at the Club. Our precious little one was now ready for Sunday school, and Saul volunteered to drop her off. Happily seeing him stepping up and taking an interest, I grew happier. One Sunday, Amelia needed something at the drugstore so she called the club for Saul to leave a message. They said that Saul was not there nor did he ever show up on Sundays for tennis. Her head began to swim as confusion once again grabbed hold. When he flew in the door, he roughly grabbed her arm and shouted, "Don't you ever check up on me again or you'll be sorry!"

One night, he was away on a business trip to New York and she was especially lonely. He never touched her anymore as intimacy was gone.

He wasn't in so she called again later. His sales manager answered, "As soon as he gets in, I'll have him call but I don't know what time."

"It's OK. I'll just wait up."

I read and stayed awake until 4 o'clock a.m. The phone rang, and it was Saul saying, "I've been out on business and you should know better than try to call. Don't do it again!" He hung up, and tears flowed to wet the pillow as trying to sleep.

When he got home, Amelia told him she did not believe his story. He was about to confront but raising the hand saying, "there is only one other way and it is to seek counseling."

He said he would go. Surprise! Hope began to grow once more. He said, "I want to see the counselor by myself."

I replied, "Fine." Saul went in alone and later Amelia. When I went into the doctor's office, I was to be kept confidential on your part.

"Of course," I replied.

"You must get your husband out of the house as soon as possible! I will go above board and recommend a lawyer today." Beginning to tremble as this was very unexpected and fearful.

"Do not wait! Please!" he said.

The imagination runs wild at words such as these, and the evidence became frightening as three days later, I found a gun at the top of his closet. Confronting Saul, he replied, "It's for our protection because of the union's threats."

"There is nothing to hear," Amelia said. "Please remove them for the children's safety."

"No!" was his reply. Trust was over, reaching the phone to call the lawyer, the games began!

This was like Olympics. It took two years just for paperwork. He blatantly went everywhere with his girlfriend. Knowledge noticed and said, "I see you ran to your safe place, didn't you?"

"Yes," Amelia replied. "I did well on my SATs. It was refreshing, and I chose GSU!" Smiling for a first in a while.

The Finale

Knowledge explains that Amelia, "having been in an exploratory existence, discovers that the quest for true love has not been found. That the men she chose wanted possession of her life and not the respect of loving. Once she loved, but after years of caring, it was ruined by the influence of money and other women who sought him out."

She still hoped that a friendship could develop, at least with opposite gender, not involving sex. This is rare. It's told but needs attention and care.

"There is one door remaining," said Knowledge. "It's the most beautiful and rich of all." Amelia walked with him around the corner and there it stood, solid gold!

Together they carefully pushed it open. It swings gently all the way back to reveal glass wrapped all the way around the room, framing the grandeur of the ocean and sky. The green water meets the magnificent white clouds and green mountains, refreshing to view. The openness of space creates the possibility to dance. There's a soft sound of a tune in the background that is pleasing to the ears. Amelia inhales and exhales with appreciation of all the senses enjoying. Sparsely scattered is the white purity of sofas and chairs of comfort. Feeling safe, she strolled back up to the window for the calm and peace it gave her. She believes she has made it to the perfect room.

"Amelia's effort have always been to be the best she could be," she thought. Her greatest gifts are her children, and she has loved them with her whole heart no matter what. Relinquishing them to their own lives, as the time to teach has passed, waiting for them to call or visit is her joy! We arrive at life naked and needy for food, bathing, and clothing. Warmth and comfort are necessary but mean little without love. There are many reasons for premature death, but usually choices are involved.

Amelia ponders, "Where does our desire for survival come from?"

When the safe world of childhood changes the young one goes inward. Living alone leaves direction of different ways spontaneously. Darkness seeks seeks and takes advantage of one's soul. To avoid that overwhelming feeling, a safe place must be found. Amelia felt safe in school and church and thoughts of an invisible father she imagined.

Knowledge knew her reading would help as she turned to writers such as Kahlil Gibran and poets Dickenson, Whitman, Shakespeare, and Rumi. Books on other religions, Buddhism, Judaism and the Christian Bible read three times. Amelia was always inquisitive. Amelia learned to leave ugliness and disrespect as a young girl and kept these principles close. Insights and love she felt from the words in these books helped her many times keep her way on the right path. This golden door represents the golden rule: "Do unto others as they do unto you." There are no "Aha!" moments, simply knowledge, experience, and reading that evolves into wisdom.

"Through Unlocked Doors" is one adventure of life. Sustaining Amelia through all this has been her friend Knowledge as her guide, cook, interrupter, and companion. Life is interesting once black and white are sorted out. It can be fun. Alive is good and so is Amelia . . . for now!

Amelia now, in her later years, has not been left entirely alone by destiny.

I Wonder

a.e.ames

I wonder about
The stars that shine
The Moon the Sun
They all are fine.

But maybe someday
They will fade
From their bright color
To a duller shade.

And if that day it ever appears
That all these things do fade
I think all that I shall not be here
As I was not when they were made.

www.ingramcontent.com/pod-product-compliance
Lightning Source LLC
LaVergne TN
LVHW041539060526
838200LV00037B/1059